·

The Light Behind the Shadows

Colleen Anthony

BALBOA.PRESS

A DIVISION OF HAY HOUSE

Balboa Press books may be ordered through booksellers or by contacting:

Balboa Press
A Division of Hay House
1663 Liberty Drive
Bloomington, IN 47403
www.balboapress.com
1 (877) 407-4847

Because of the dynamic nature of the Internet, any web addresses or links contained in this book may have changed since publication and may no longer be valid. The views expressed in this work are solely those of the author and do not necessarily reflect the views of the publisher, and the publisher hereby disclaims any responsibility for them.

The author of this book does not dispense medical advice or prescribe the use of any technique as a form of treatment for physical, emotional, or medical problems without the advice of a physician, either directly or indirectly. The intent of the author is only to offer information of a general nature to help you in your quest for emotional and spiritual well-being. In the event you use any of the information in this book for yourself, which is your constitutional right, the author and the publisher assume no responsibility for your actions.

Any people depicted in stock imagery provided by Adobe Stock Images are models, and such images are being used for illustrative purposes only.
Certain stock imagery © Adobe Stock Images

Print information available on the last page.

Scripture quotations marked NKJV are taken from the New King James Version®. Copyright © 1982 by Thomas Nelson. Used by permission. All rights reserved.

Scripture quotations marked NIV are taken from The Holy Bible, New International Version®, NIV®. Copyright © 1973, 1978, 1984, 2011 by Biblica, Inc.® Used by permission. All rights reserved worldwide.

Scripture quotations marked KJV are taken from the King James Version.

Scripture quotations marked NLT are taken from the Holy Bible, New Living Translation, Copyright © 1996, 2004, 2015 by Tyndale House Foundation. Used by permission of Tyndale House Publishers, Inc., Carol Stream, Illinois 60188. All rights reserved.

Scripture quotations marked ESV taken from The Holy Bible, English Standard Version® (ESV®), Copyright © 2001 by Crossway, a publishing ministry of Good News Publishers. All rights reserved.

ISBN: 978-1-9822-4393-7 (sc)
ISBN: 978-1-9822-4395-1 (hc)
ISBN: 978-1-9822-4394-4 (e)

Library of Congress Control Number: 2020903930

Balboa Press rev. date: 03/04/2020

CONTENTS

DEDICATION

Our days on earth are like a shadow.
—1 Chronicles 29:15 (NIV)

I dedicate this book to my Lord and Savior Jesus Christ, who has given me life here on earth and an eternal home in heaven. He has promised to never leave me or forsake me, and He has walked through every storm of life with me. May this book bring Him honor and glory, and may those that read it be drawn to Him.

ACKNOWLEDGMENTS

A heartfelt thank you to:

❖ My husband, Eric. Thank you for staying by my side through all the storms and trials of life. Your steadfastness and leadership have been a blessing from above! Thank you for all that you do for our family and for the blessing you are to so many. I thank God for you, and I love you dearly!

❖ My daughter, Marti Lynn. What an amazing blessing you are to your dad and me. Thank you for your faithful service in helping us through so many hard times. Thank you for helping edit this book and your wise input. Your love for Jesus and your gentle spirit are a sweet fragrance to our family and to this world. Your friendship is one of my treasured blessings, and I love you so much!

❖ My beloved sisters, Mary Lynn Brown (now with Jesus) and Martha Wagner. Thank you for your love and forever friendship. What a blessing you both have been to me! I cannot even imagine what life would have been like had we not had each other. I am forever grateful to God for the wonderful friendship He gave us. I am so thankful that we will all spend eternity together and never be separated again. I love you both!

❖ My cousin, Jonathan LaBenne, and his wife, Pamela, for their generosity in blessing me with this book publishing package.

You are a direct answer to prayer. Thank you for your love and support as well as all the prayers. I value our friendship greatly! *(Check out Jon's amazing, God-given talent at his website, www. jonathanbearman.com.)*

❖ My cousin, Joshua LaBenne. God has blessed you with an incredible talent. Thank you for sharing it with me! Your original painting is the perfect piece for the book cover. *(Check out Josh's website, www.joshlabenne.com.)*

❖ My niece, Jennifer. Thank you, dear Jen, for your help with writing concepts and all the edits. You are amazing, and I love you dearly!

❖ My cousin, Karen Cedarland. Thank you for your amazing proofreading skills and support in helping get this manuscript to the publisher. You are a gift and a treasure!

❖ To all of my prayer warriors who faithfully prayed for this project over the last five years. You all are an amazing blessing to me!

❖ And most importantly of all, my deepest thanks to my Savior Jesus Christ who has carried me through all the storms of life. Thank You, Lord, for my life here on earth and for the one to come in heaven. Thank You for being Sovereign God and for doing all things right! We anxiously await Your soon return!

FOREWORD

Why write a book? I am not a writer and have never had a desire to be one. Yet, in the spring of 2014 while battling breast cancer, people repeatedly said, "You need to share your story." I kept brushing the thought off, thinking, *Why would I do that? Everyone has trials, and my story is no different or special than anyone else's. There are many others who have been through greater trials than I have been through.* However, the comments kept coming. One day in the shower while washing my bald head, I was pondering the idea of sharing my story, and I wondered if God was trying to tell me something. If He was, I did not want to miss that blessing, and so I decided I had better pray about this. On April 8, 2014, I wrote in my prayer journal: "Lord, if You want to share my story, I'm okay with that, but You will have to write it."

The answer came on May 17, 2014, just thirty-nine days later. While in Jackson, Wyoming, celebrating my husband's birthday, we decided to stop in for a quick visit with my cousin Jon and his wife, Pam. While sitting in their living room, I whipped off my cowboy scarf that hid my very bald head and said, "Hey, Jon, how do you like my new hairdo?"

His sobered response was, "Wow, Cousin. I sure hope you are going to share your story in a book."

I responded, "I don't know, but I'm praying about it." Jon had no idea what I had written in my prayer journal, and I didn't share it with him.

A few minutes later he said, "I want to give you a publishing package. I bought three, and I didn't really know why—but now I do."

I was shocked! Wow! What a direct answer to my prayer. I now had a complete publishing package all paid for. Unbelievable! I could never have dreamed up such a thing. On the way home that night, my daughter said, "Mom, if you were waiting for a sign from God on whether to share your story or not, I think you just got hit over the head!" Thank You, Lord, for such a direct answer to my prayer.

The following night I was discussing the book idea with my daughter and mentioned that I did not want the book to be about me but rather about what God has done in my life. I wanted the title to reflect that. My daughter's response was, "You could title it *The Light Behind the Shadows* in reference to what Grandpa said."

Over and over again before my brain surgery, the verse that came to me was, "Yea though I walk through the valley of the shadow of death, I will fear no evil; for You are with me" (Psalm 23:14 NKJV). My dad had shared with me during that time that it takes light to make a shadow. The verse says the *shadow of death* because God is there. He is the light. Jesus walks through the *valley of the shadow of death* with us. He is the light that has conquered death. We are never alone. If He was not there, then that verse would read "through the valley of death" instead of the "shadow of death." What a comfort to know Him and to know He is with us.

The next morning after this discussion, when the publisher called and said, "Jon LaBenne has transferred this ISBN number into your name, and we need a title for the book," I had one. God has been with me through this entire project. It has been a journey of faith for me, and it has had many trials along the way. I have buried so many loved ones during this last five years and had many disappointments, but God is faithful and has been with me every step of the way. He is truly the light behind all the shadows in my life.

I hope as you read this book, you will let Jesus minister to your soul. Life is brief, and eternity is forever. Let Jesus partner with you, and accept His plan of salvation if you haven't already. Heaven is going to be amazing, and I hope I will meet you there. If you are already a Christian but discouraged and maybe offended at God, let Him change your paradigm. He is good and loves you so much. Let Him be Lord of your life, and you will find it is the only way to live victoriously.

SECTION 1
RESETTING THE SAIL

I am the good shepherd; the
good shepherd gives His life for the sheep.

—John 10:11 (NKJV)

A Paradigm Shift

I have been crucified with Christ; it is no longer I who live, but Christ lives in me; and the life I now live in the flesh I live by faith in the Son of God, who loved me and gave Himself up for me.

—Galatians 2:20 (NKJV)

It was one of those classic small-town hardware stores where you could find about anything you needed from kitchen utensils to paint. I found myself there in January 1998, and I was there not to purchase anything but to meet someone. Her name was Doris, and we shared a mutual friend. Doris and her husband were the owners of the hardware store in a small town in central Washington, not too far from where we lived at the time. A mutual friend had told me, "You really need to meet Doris. I think you would be great friends." So shortly after her suggestion, I decided to stop in and introduce myself to her. Our friend was right—we did enjoy a great friendship. More than twenty years ago, God had set up a divine appointment for me, and I was unaware of the powerful impact it would have on my life. I was about to witness Galatians 2:20 in real life.

Not long after our friendship started, Doris found out her breast cancer had returned and had spread throughout her body. She was now dealing with a very aggressive, malignant brain tumor. She and her husband had just finished building their dream home on the ridge behind our ranch. Life for them had just taken a nasty turn! I was heartbroken for them and madly praying for a miracle.

The disease moved quickly, and her condition declined rapidly. I had been tracking her progress through our mutual friend and one day decided to stop in for a visit. I was warned by her caregivers that her condition was poor and that her body had really taken a beating. I had no idea what I was walking into.

I entered their beautiful new dream home, nestled in the pine trees, and was admiring the grandeur of the construction when my eyes caught sight of my friend Doris. She was sitting alone on the couch across the room. I was speechless, and I am sure my face showed my disbelief. She was a rack of bones, and one eyelid was sown shut. The other eye was still open but grossly protruding out of the socket. There was a small piece of plastic wrap over the eye to keep it from drying out. The cancer had taken over, and her life was coming to an end. Here sat a beautiful, classy woman whom I no longer recognized. She called out, "Who's there?"

Her caregiver answered, "Doris, it's Colleen Anthony."

Her response was something I will never forget. Her first words to me were, "Oh, Colleen, God is so good!"

I was speechless but thought to myself, *Good? Are you kidding me? How could this be good?* I know God is good by His very nature but to have that be her first words stunned me. Doris was not focused on herself but on God's love and care for her. I was fighting back the tears and not sure what to say. I was not thinking the same thing. I sat down across from her, but I do not even remember what we talked about. I do not remember anything other than I wanted to throw up. I was amazed at the peace she had in the midst of this terrible storm. There was no bitterness, no self-pity, no complaining, and no worries. She was glorifying God in the flames of this trial. I told her I was praying and that I loved her. I went out and climbed into my pickup, put my head on the steering wheel, and wept. I cried for a long time as this scene had about unhinged me. Later that day, God spoke to me through a song titled "Trust His Heart" by Babbie Y. Mason. The chorus goes like this:

> God is too wise to be mistaken,
> God is too good to be unkind,
> So when you don't understand
> When you don't see His plan
> When you can't trace His hand
> Trust His heart.

Shortly after my visit, Doris passed away and went to be with Jesus. Doris had made her reservation in heaven. She had accepted God's plan for her salvation, and her sins were paid for by Jesus's death on the cross. I knew by her testimony that she was ready to depart from planet Earth. Our friendship was short-lived, but it had a great impact on my life. I was forever changed by what I had just seen and heard.

One of her close friends shared at her funeral how Doris had lost the ability to speak at the end, but she could see through a tiny slit in her eyelid, so she would communicate in writing. During those last few days of life, her friend hovered over her face and said, "Doris, your body is a mess! Are you doing okay in there?"

Doris responded by writing, "God is so close to me."

Almost everything had been taken away, but she had Jesus and that was enough. The Holy Spirit was right there with her and was giving her supernatural strength to endure to the end. Her friend went on to say that Doris lived out her favorite verse, Galatians 2:20. She said Doris interpreted this verse in a personal way, and she would read like this:

> I, Doris, choose to die to the pulls of this world, die
> to the lusts for power, money, and any temporary
> pleasures this world has to offer. As long as I, Doris,
> live in this physical body here on this earth ruled by
> sin and Satan and in these dimensions ruled by time,

I choose to trust God to show me where and what real truth and happiness are. So I put my faith in God's eternal truth, not the empty promises of this temporary world. And because God chose to become a man and dwell among us—yet a man without sin—He became my perfect Savior. Then He allowed all my sin to be laid on Him, and then He died for my sin so now I do not have to die and be separated from God. Now I, Doris, because of the salvation that my Savior offered me, am free to know love and to be loved by my God, my Savior. And my life will be lived for God's eternal purposes, not mine.

Her friend went on to say:

Doris wanted God to get the glory for any good thing that she became. She lived her life to be an example of what God would do in anyone's life if they would allow Him to. Doris showed us all that there is a God and He made it possible for us to find Him through His letter to us, the Bible. God is not just an energy force of nature; He is living, personal, and loving. Doris wanted us to know that He is full of compassion and He has mercy on our fallen condition. She desires us to know that God wants to set us free so much that He even paid the price for our sin because we were not able to do it ourselves. He has given us everything we need to find Him and be united to Him. But it is our choice if we want to join God or not. Doris chose to trust God, and then she showed us how to do it. Doris wanted her memorial service to be a day of hope for you. That was her prayer; that was her life.

Doris's illness and passing had a profound effect on my life. I realize now that our meeting was a divine appointment orchestrated by God.

He allowed me a front-row seat in the concert hall of her life. Just like an eagle in a storm, Doris allowed the winds of adversity to lift her up. She turned her storm clouds into a chariot. I watched her rise above the storm of this disease. I watched her leave planet Earth, glorifying God all the way. I watched her live what she believed.

It has been almost twenty years since Doris passed away. She set an incredible example for me without even knowing it on how to weather the storms of life with God at the helm. She had no idea what was up ahead for me, but God knew and was faithfully preparing me for the storms that were brewing on the horizon and headed my way.

Just prior to meeting Doris, I had been attending a series of seminars for my job called Peak Performers Network. Every month we would attend a seminar and hear from different motivational speakers. During one of those events, I learned about paradigm shifts. A paradigm is defined as a collection of thoughts, behaviors, and perceptions that dictate your feelings, actions, and results. A paradigm shift is an important change that happens when the usual way of thinking about or doing something is replaced by a new and different way.

Another concept they taught us was the idea of resetting our life sail. If we were to change our compass course just three degrees when navigating a sailboat, it might not be very obvious at first, but after several hours or days of sailing, the change of course would be significant. The change can be so significant that we can end up in a completely different harbor. The message conveyed that if we change our views, we can change our lives. Change our paradigms, and we will change the results of our lives. Both of these phrases where used in a business application, but God was about to use this as a spiritual application in my life.

It was also explained that the mind has two parts: the conscious and subconscious. The conscious mind, which is the thinking mind (the intellect or educated mind), has the ability to accept or reject information. The subconscious mind, which is the emotional mind, can only accept information and is unable to reject what comes in. When information is fed into the conscious mind, you either accept it or reject it. Like a one-way valve, what is accepted goes into the subconscious part of the brain and becomes what you believe whether it is right or wrong. The problem is that people often do not correctly filter what comes in and will accept information that is not true. Sometimes people don't filter what comes in, and then information goes straight to the subconscious and becomes fact.

The scary thing about the subconscious mind is that it cannot determine the difference between that which is real (truth) and that which is imagined (untrue), and it becomes what is called a paradigm. People who are abused or bullied often have a wrong paradigm about themselves. They have no self-esteem or self-worth because the subconscious was fed false information. The paradigm is what produces results in a person's life whether good or bad. It is what travels down into a person's actions and behaviors. It is what comes out of a person when life events squeeze him or her. A person reacts based on what is in their paradigm.

God was about to start a paradigm shift in my theology. He was about to change my view of who He is and of life here on earth. He started to redirect my life sail, and at first, it did not seem like there was much of a change. Looking back over my life, the change has been significant and has completely redirected my course.

After witnessing Doris's journey, I realized that her focus was different than mine. Doris was not saying that this trial was good but rather that God was good in the trial. She had her eyes on God rather than on herself or her circumstances. She was looking at Him and His goodness, not on herself. She was not blaming God for her disease. His plan was much bigger than hers, and she had accepted that. God could have healed her down here on earth, but instead, He healed her in heaven. Her work was done, and she was about to experience a major first-class upgrade. She is now in the presence of her Lord, completely healed and completely happy. She is now in a place of perfection where there is no more pain, disease, death, or sorrow. Doris has arrived!

The Holy Spirit of God was living on the inside of her, giving her supernatural strength and peace. He gave her the ability to rise above the storm. She experienced real joy. Joy is different than being happy. Joy is that genuine contentment that is deep down inside. Doris saw God in the darkness of this trial and embraced Him. He was her light behind the shadows.

Trials in our lives can produce twenty million questions. We often wonder, *Why is this happening? Why me? Why them? This doesn't seem fair!* There are so many things we just do not understand. I questioned why God chose to take Doris so early. I wanted her to live, and I knew she wanted to live. I believed God could heal her. She was still so young. In all honesty, I was not seeing the *good* just then, and it was hard to be on the same page as Doris.

I was born and raised in a Christian home and taught from the Bible at an early age. I believed God to be my Creator, and I had invited Him into my life to be my Savior at a very young age. I did not want to go to hell, and I knew that I needed to ask Him for forgiveness of my sins. My salvation was not based on my good works but rather on accepting God's free gift of salvation. I was confident that I would go to heaven if I died, but I did not have the close, Spirit-filled relationship with Jesus like Doris had.

I knew all the right things to say to sound spiritual, but the truth was it was all just head knowledge and not heart knowledge. I believed Jesus died to give us a relationship with Himself. The Lord wanted to walk through life with me and guide me each step of the way. He wanted me to live with the power to rise above my circumstances and to live victorious no matter what happened to me. He wanted to be my companion, my advisor, and my friend. He also wanted to be the Lord of my life. However, I was concerned with what would come out of me if I were squeezed like Doris. Would I be praising God in the flames? Was my paradigm about God and life here on earth correct? I know I had the salvation part right, but what about that victorious living and rising above the storm part?

Just before I met Doris, I had asked to be rebaptized. I had been baptized around the age of five, but I was not fully aware of what I was doing. In March 1997, I stood up in front of our church and declared publicly that Jesus was my Savior and I wanted Him to be the Lord of my life. I had been listening to some ministry tapes on the lordship of Christ, and I had been convicted that this was something I wanted to experience, although I was a bit afraid of what that might involve. However, I was committed and asked God to help me. Ten months later, I met Doris. God was beginning to do a major paradigm shift in my life. He was about to show me what the lordship of Christ looked like.

Sadly, at that time in my life, I viewed Christianity as something to keep me out of hell and as a religion that served me rather than transformed me. I did not see God as the one who knew what was best for me. I thought I had it all figured out and would just consult with Him when needed. My eyes were focused on myself. I was as good as my circumstances. I had the *cruise ship* mentality where life is smooth sailing and all you want is there for the taking. I wanted to do things my way and have God answer my prayers the way I wanted them answered. I had my salvation ticket to heaven, but I wanted my dream filled life here on earth too.

Prayer to me was more like a vending machine where I would feed in my request and then expected the desire to be granted. For example, if there was something I really wanted, I would pray that I would get it instead of praying whether it was God's will for me to have it. I prayed about things, but it was just for things I wanted Him to do or fix, not communing with Him as my guide or counselor and most of all as

Sovereign God. With regard to Doris, I was not praying for God's will to be done but rather that she would be healed and live longer. It never occurred to me that He might have more blessing in her death than her life down here, and it didn't occur to me that Doris was getting an upgrade. I was looking at her disease with its devastating effects along with her needs and desires, and I wanted her to stay. However, God is in control, and He had a much bigger plan. His plan was for Doris to join Him.

I had the salvation part, but I was not allowing Christ to be the Lord of my life. I was not allowing Him into every detail of my life. I would allow Him into some areas but was not fully surrendered in other areas. I was afraid to let Him control everything. What if He asked me to do something I did not want to do or give up something I wanted to keep? Would I have been able to honestly say like Doris, "God is good," and, "I surrender all," if my body was torn apart like hers and my dreams and everything I held dear was ripped out of my fingers? I did not have that kind of faith. I knew that Doris could honestly sing the song "All to Jesus I surrender, All to Him I freely give, I will ever love and trust Him, In His presence daily live" (by Judson W. Van de Venter). She truly was surrendered and gave everything up to Jesus, trusting Him with her life. She understood and knew that Jesus loved her, and she, in turn, loved Him. They were friends, and He was with her every step of the way. She was living her theme verse: "it is no longer I who live, but Christ lives in me" (Galatians 2:20 NKJV). Did Doris like what was happening in her life? No, not for a minute! I believe she prayed to be healed and wanted to live. Her death was hard, and she suffered physically. The difference was her perspective. She accepted that God was in control of her life and that her destiny was a forever home in heaven with Jesus. She had her eyes on Him, not herself. She trusted Him!

God could have healed Doris, but she had finished her work here, and He was calling her home to heaven. Doris is now in the physical presence of her Lord and more alive today than she has ever been. What an amazing thing to think about. She has been healed and set free and will live in a sinless, perfect environment forever.

Corrie Ten Boom once said: "For a child of God, death is only a passing through to a wonderful new world."

This paradigm shift that God started in my theology continued over the years following my friendship with Doris. The life storms that were brewing on the horizon did come and swept over my life with great force. Without God's presence and help in my life, I would have surely capsized.

I did not really understand what all God was trying to teach me until I was squeezed. It is those storms in life that really start to reveal what it is we truly believe and what we are focused on. When the unexpected gales blow and the pain is so great we cannot breathe, our emotional subconscious paradigms show up.

It is amazing how we can sympathize with others and pray for them and give them all kinds of advice when they are going through a life storm, but then when it is our health or loss, it is so different, and God has our full attention. I watched Doris suffer and grieved her passing, but so much of my life came into focus for me when I heard those heart-stopping words: "Your pathology shows cancer." When it is us facing the giant or when we receive that heart-shattering news that a loved one is gone, it is then we find out if that head knowledge is really heart knowledge.

It is false to think that as followers of Jesus, nothing bad should happen to us because God is on our side. We often expect Him to fix everything when we pray. He does come to our aid and can fix things when we call upon Him, but the answers are not always the answers we were expecting. It is amazing how often we have this false paradigm and don't even realize it. We are promised in the Bible that we will have trials.

> In the world you will have tribulation; but be of good
> cheer, I have overcome the world. (John 16:33 NKJV)

The Bible is full of stories of those who suffered through great trials in life. In the Old Testament, Daniel was thrown into the lions' den for praying. God delivered him, but he still had to spend the night with the hungry lions. There were the three men thrown into the fiery furnace for being faithful to God and not bowing down to idols. They were spared, but they still went through the fire. Job suffered terrible loss even though he was considered a righteous man. God restored everything to him and more, but he still went through personal loss and sorrow. Joseph's life was another story that doesn't seem to make sense. He was betrayed several times over and spent years in prison after being wrongly accused. At the right time, God delivered him and put him in a place of authority. The same is true in the New Testament of Jesus's followers who suffered loss and went through trial after trial. Life doesn't always go the way we want it to. It's a wrong paradigm to think otherwise.

God's perspective is so much different than ours. This world is a war zone, and we need His help to make it through. Our lives will end someday, so why is it we think it's all about the here and now? Our paradigm will change when we focus on what the Bible tells us is coming for those who put their trust in the Lord. God clearly tells us in the Bible there is life after death. For those who have accepted His plan, there is a future in heaven free of sin, sickness, disease, death, and separation. I am so thankful that because of what Jesus accomplished by dying on the cross, I will, like Doris, go to heaven. I will not get to heaven on my good performance but because of what Jesus has done for me. We are saved by the grace and mercy of God. It is His plan of salvation, not ours. We get to heaven by His righteousness, not our own. I believe these things are true and know I will someday see Doris again. We will be friends forever because life will never end. How amazing is that!?

> For by grace you have been saved through faith,
> and that not of yourselves; it is the gift of God,
> not of works, lest anyone should boast.
>
> —Ephesians 2:8-9 (NKJV)

Disappointment—His Appointment

by Edith Lillian Young

"Disappointment—His Appointment"
Change one letter, then I see
That the thwarting of my purpose
Is God's better choice for me.
His appointment must be blessing,
Tho' it may come in disguise,
For the end from the beginning
Open to His wisdom lies.
"Disappointment—His Appointment"
Whose? The Lord, who loves me best,
Understands and knows me fully,
Who my faith and love would test;
For, like loving earthly parent,
He rejoices when He knows
That His child accepts, unquestioned,
All that from His wisdom flows.
"Disappointment—His Appointment"
"No good thing will He withhold,"
From denials oft we gather
Treasures of His love unfold,
Well He knows each broken purpose
Leads to fuller, deeper trust,
And the end of all His dealings
Proves our God is wise and just.
"Disappointment—His Appointment"
Lord, I take it, then as such.

Like the clay in hands of potter,
Yielding wholly to Thy touch.
All my life's plan in Thy moulding,
Not one single choice be mine;
Let me answer, unrepining—
"Father, not my will, but Thine."

2

BITTER OR BETTER

And blessed is he who is not offended because of Me.
—Matthew 11:6 (NKJV)

I heard a story of young man who was getting ready to graduate from college. For many months prior to his graduation, he had been admiring a beautiful sports car in a dealer's showroom. His wealthy father could afford to buy him this car, and so he let it be known that was what he wanted for his graduation gift. Graduation day came, and the father called his son to his private study and told him how proud he was of him and how much he loved him. He then handed him a beautifully wrapped gift box. The son opened the gift and found a beautiful, leather-bound Bible with his name embossed in gold on the front cover. He became angry with his father and yelled, "With all of your money, why would you give me a Bible rather than the sports car that I wanted?" He then stormed out, leaving the Bible and his father behind.

Many years passed, and the young man had moved on and was successful in business. He had a beautiful home and family of his own. One day he was thinking how old his father was, and because he had not seen him for years, he decided that perhaps he should go for a visit. However, before he could plan the trip, a call came informing him of his father's passing. His father had left his entire estate to him, and now the attorney was requesting that he come immediately to take care of business.

When the son arrived at his father's house, sadness and regret filled his heart. He began to search through his father's important documents and saw the Bible his father had given him. It looked just as new as the day he received it. With tears, he opened it up and saw a verse that his father had carefully underlined. It read: "And if you then, being evil, know how to give good gifts to your children, how much more will your Father who is in heaven give good gifts to those who ask Him!" (Matthew 7:11 NKJV).

As the son was reading this verse, a car key fell out from the back of the Bible. The key had a tag on it that read "PAID IN FULL" along with the dealer's name where the sports car had been so many years ago. What a paradigm shift this son must have had at that moment. He had wasted many years being bitter toward his father who loved him dearly. Now his father was gone, along with the opportunity to make things right.

So many times in life we miss God's blessings because they are not packaged as we expected them to be. A bitter disappointment or a loss can cause us to turn away from God, and we completely miss the blessing that was hidden in the trial.

Devastating news can come that reveals you have cancer or your job was terminated or your spouse is going to leave you for someone else. Maybe a loved one was taken that you were begging God to heal or your kids have turned their backs on you. When we get hit with a tragedy or disappointment like this, we are faced with the decision of how we will respond.

These gut-wrenching blows can make us angry, fearful, hopeless, or maybe resentful. What do we do when the storms of life come up against us and we are battered by the waves of life? What happens when we get that horrible piece of news that leaves us weak in the knees and sick to our stomachs? This is where our paradigms are revealed. If we do not truly understand or believe in who God is, we might blame

Him for the tragedy or become offended by Him because He did not prevent it or answer our prayers the way we wanted Him to. We might shake our fists at Him and become bitter or indifferent. These painful trials in life are what really test our faith. Do we believe God is good and that He loves us?

When we find ourselves staring at disappointments or tragedy in life, we are faced with which fork in the road to take. The better way turns us toward God, while the bitter way will turn us away from God. Sometimes we think we have no choice, and we let our emotions have complete control. However, we do have choices. It is so easy to let our emotions rule our behaviors, especially when we get hurt or we do not get our own way. It is especially hard when we are doubled over in grief. The only way to manage our emotions successfully is to allow God to help and that is by turning toward Him.

If our belief system is flawed and we have allowed false information into the subconscious (emotional mind), then we will react based on what is programmed in. If we do not believe that God loves us, then we will doubt His love when things go wrong. If we have a wrong view of who God is, then we will be offended or angry at Him and maybe blame Him for the storms that come our way.

Turning toward God brings healing, comfort, peace, and blessing. It brings God into the picture, and He helps us through. He can turn a mess into a message, a test into a testimony, a trial into a triumph, and a victim into a victory. He is able to heal a broken heart and mend our shattered emotions. The problem is we often push Him away because we are offended at Him or have unmet expectations. I can tell you firsthand that I have tried to manage my emotions both with God and without God. I have taken both the bitter road and the better road in life at different times, and I have learned the hard way that becoming bitter and angry is not the answer. Turning toward God is the only way to sail through the storms of this life.

Turning away from God brings just the opposite of turning towards Him. It brings more pain, fear, loneliness, stress, misery, and defeat. It brings the need to seek out other things to deaden the pain like alcohol or drugs. This bitter fork in the road is where we can so easily throw in the towel and say, "This prayer thing just doesn't work." Our expectations are again a vending machine approach to God. We feed in our prayer and expect to get the item we requested. The problem is prayer doesn't work that way. God hears our requests and then decides what is best according to His plan. Prayer is a conversation with a loving Father who cares for us. He knows exactly what to do, and sometimes it is not at all what we want or expect.

We are often tempted to take the bitter way because it is where our emotions want to go. We decide to do life as we see best and leave God out of the picture. It's in our nature to play the blame game, and we soon spiral out of control when nothing in life seems to be working in our favor. Over time, this bitter path can lead to self-destruction.

There are two stories in the Bible that have helped me in understanding how to face disappointment and unmet expectations. In Matthew 11, we read about John the Baptist, a close friend of Jesus. He was doing what he was sent to do and was proclaiming that the Messiah was coming. He was telling the world help was on the way. He had faith in what had been foretold by the prophets in the Old Testament and believed that Jesus was coming to make all things right. But John was unjustly accused and cast into prison.

It was in prison while awaiting his execution that he sent word to Jesus and asked, "Are you the coming One or do we look for another?" (Matthew 11:3 NKJV). John wrestled with doubts when his life went upside down. He was going to be killed. Why wasn't Jesus delivering him? Jesus sent word back and said, "Go and tell John the things which you hear and see: the blind see and the lame walk; the lepers are cleansed and the deaf hear; the dead are raised up and the poor have the gospel preached to them. And blessed is he who is not offended because of Me" (Matthew 11:4–6 NKJV). What must have gone through John's mind? This was the Jesus of whom John said, "Behold! The Lamb of God, who takes away the sin of the world" (John 1:29 NKJV).

What a test this must have been for John. Did he really trust this one he had been proclaiming? John's head was about to roll, and his friend was going to let this happen. On top of it all, Jesus sent word telling him not to be offended. Seriously?! John was not planning on an early death, especially this kind of death. Jesus could have just spoken a word or sent an angel. He was a miracle worker, after all. John had a choice to make—to believe or not believe.

John's work was complete, and he had fulfilled his purpose here on earth. His trials would soon be behind him, and he would be safely home in heaven. John's life would be over before he knew the whole story. Jesus had not yet been crucified, and so I think John might have seen his deliverance coming another way. Jesus did save John, but it was through His death on the cross and His resurrection from the grave that conquered death forever. When John proclaimed, "Behold the Lamb of God!" he never would have thought it would end this way. John was faithful, but it cost him his life.

This Must be the Lamb

by Michael Card

On a gray April morning as a chilling wind blew,
A thousand dark promises were about to come true.
As Satan stood trembling knowing now he had lost,
As the Lamb took His first step on the way to the cross.

They mocked His true calling and laughed at His fate,
So glad to see the Gentle One consumed by their hate.
Unaware of the wind and the darkening sky,
So blind to the fact that it was God limping by.

Another Bible story in Luke 24 tells of two disciples of Jesus who were walking on the road to Emmaus right after Jesus was crucified. They were downcast and discouraged by the way they saw things turning out. Jesus had proclaimed He was the Messiah, the Son of God. Now He was dead, or at least that is what these two disciples were thinking. Nothing made sense to them, and they were very discouraged. However, Jesus had conquered death. He had risen from the grave and now had come alongside them on that road and they were discussing these things with Him. They did not expect to see Him and did not recognize Him. Jesus expounded to them all the scriptures concerning Himself. When they got near the village where they were going, they invited Him to stay with them. As He sat at the table with them, He took bread, blessed and broke it, and gave it to them. God opened their eyes; they recognized Him, and He vanished from their sight. Can you imagine the extreme shift of emotions they must have felt? They went from the hopeless grief of watching Jesus crucified to the extreme joy of seeing Him alive. Now they realized He had conquered death just like He said He would. As followers of Jesus, they would live forever in heaven. Death and hell had no power over them. Talk about a paradigm shift!

These two accounts show that even those who were with Jesus in person struggled with how to respond to major disappointments. The two disciples had seen Jesus face-to-face and knew Him as their friend. They had seen His miracles and believed He was the Messiah. You would think that having walked and talked with Jesus, it would be easier to trust in Him, but they still struggled. John the Baptist was the one who prepared the way for the Messiah and boldly proclaimed He had come, yet while in prison, he wondered if what he had said was really true. These stories have comforted me because I have struggled in life with major disappointments and losses. I have questioned God's ways and wondered why things have happened to me. I believe everyone struggles at one time or another in the hard places of their lives.

My nephew Michael faced a huge disappointment in life several years ago. He was diagnosed in his early twenties with multiple sclerosis. He was married and living in Hawaii with a very successful career. His disease did not progress until his mid-thirties. During the summer of 2014, while I was going through breast cancer treatment, I had the privilege of spending some quality time with him while he was visiting us in Idaho. He was bound to his wheelchair and only had the use of one hand and could slightly move his head. Mike has a joyful, positive spirit despite his handicap, which displays such a wonderful testimony to God's grace in his life. We sat on the porch one day and had a long discussion about the trials and disappointments of life.

Shortly after returning home from our visit, I received this email from him.

Dear Aunt Colleen,

It was so good to get to see you this last week. ... I was getting pretty weak by the end of the trip there and wanted to clarify some of the things I said. I encouraged you to "let go", "letting go" is the hardest thing I have ever done. I always thought it meant "giving up". ... I am finding it does not. As I've had to let go of the things I thought were so important I am finding that God replaces them with things that are far better. Three or four years ago I started dragging my left leg. Stairs became a bigger problem. My office was on the second floor of a building that did not have an elevator. At first, I just noticed it took more effort to get upstairs. I would often stop enjoy a cup of coffee on the landing and pretend I was just enjoying the view. Within months it would take me almost an hour to get up those two flights of stairs. People would see me struggling and stop and ask if they could help ... I never accepted help. I struggled on sure that I could overcome this. I had built my dream business on the most beautiful island I could find, and I was not going to let this MS stop me now.

The Lord has removed every prop and form of support that I was relying on. I kept thinking this could not possibly get worse. Certainly I can adapt and I can figure out a way to make a good life for myself, but the losses kept coming. It culminated with my experience with the H1N1 flu in January. It hit incredibly hard and fast. I remember waking up and feeling like I was dying. I heard this rattling in my chest and realized there was no toughing this one out. The next few days were surreal. Several times I knew I was very close to death. The Lord gave me the very real sense that it was my choice if I wanted to stay or to go. I chose to stay. My life has been radically different since that experience. None of the things that I was sure I needed to be happy are available to me anymore, naturally speaking, my future looks a little bleak but, I have more peace and I am happier than I have ever been. I believe this is because I have finally "let go." I let go of my plans, my ideas, my ambitions. In doing so, I am finding the Lord to be providing in ways I could not have imagined. Instead of grieving the things I have lost I recognize what a gift life is even in my compromised condition. How blessed I am by my loving family. What an incredible future we have to look forward to.

I just wanted to reach out and make sure you know how much I love and respect you. You are in the fight of your life, I am in the fight of mine. The Lord has brought me to the point where I recognize that I must simply surrender. I am not giving up, I love life ... I would never encourage you to give up.

I love you,
M

I lay my "whys?" before Your cross in worship kneeling,
My mind beyond all hope, my heart beyond all feeling;
And worshipping, realize that I in knowing You, don't need a "why?"

—Ruth Bell Graham

Michael has been forced to stand at this bitter or better fork in the road of life and decide how to respond. He has chosen the better way and turned toward God. God has given him the strength to endure through the Holy Spirit living inside him. Even though Mike's circumstances have not improved he is still happy. He has his eyes fixed on his eternal home in heaven where all things will be made right and he will be healthy and whole again. Mike's condition has continued to decline, and all that he can move now are his eyes and mouth. I recently spent some time with him, and one of the first things he said to me was, "Aunt, we have so much to be thankful for." Wow! What a perspective. Mike's eyes are fixed on his Savior and the life to come in heaven. Just like Doris, he sees the goodness of God while in the midst of the flames.

My dad was another amazing example to me on how to face the disappointments of life. He was one of the most positive people I have ever known. Dad had four types of cancer over his eighty-nine years of life, and he graciously embraced each illness with a calm resolve that God was in control. He had a hilarious sense of humor and would keep us doubled over in laughter even when he was sick. He was one of my heroes. He served in World War II as a medic and earned the Silver Star for bravery when he risked his life to save the life of another. He had a deep love for God and a strong conviction to share the gospel message with his fellow soldiers. I am sure that there were many men in heaven who thanked him when he arrived for sharing God's amazing plan of salvation with them before they were killed during those days of brutal combat in the South Pacific. Dad saw many of his comrades die on the battlefield. He was faithful and not ashamed or fearful to share his faith with all who were suffering.

Dad was a member of some of the first glider troops to land in Japan after the atomic bomb fell releasing its dangerous toxins. My dad was exposed to the radiation from the bomb and was most likely affected by it. It is not known if that was the cause of his multiple kinds of cancer, but to him, it did not matter because he trusted God with his life. The final cancer started in his prostate and moved into the bones, eventually taking him from us.

Toward the end of his life, I traveled to Washington to be with my parents and help them out. One night while I was there, my dad woke up in extreme pain. I do not think he had slept much, and I found him very early in the morning sitting in his recliner in the living room. I asked how he was doing, and his response was, "It was kind of a rough night, but you know, we need to look for the positive or bright things today and minimize the dark things. Focus on what is good today. God's presence in our life makes all the difference. He makes a way through the dark times." What an outlook. What example to follow. He encouraged me to look beyond the circumstances and see the good in all situations. According to Charles Spurgeon, "Any man can sing in the day but only God can give songs in the night."

On a lighter note, I enjoyed a story that emphasized the difference our perspective can make. A woman was going through chemo, and when she woke up one morning, she found that she only had 3 hairs left on her head. "Well," she said, "I think I'll braid my hair today," which she did, and she had a great day. The next morning she only had two hairs, and so she decided to part it in the middle, and she had another great day. The third day she was down to one hair so it was time for a ponytail, and she had a fun, fun day. The next morning when she looked into the mirror, she discovered that she had no hair at all. "Yay!" she exclaimed. "I do not need to fix my hair today." Although this is a humorous story, the message to me was profound. We get to choose our outlooks and our attitudes about things. What are we focusing on? Are we looking at the good or the bad? Do we focus on eternal life or the life that's going to soon end? Are we focused on what God is doing or on what Satan is doing? Are we focused on what is important to us or on what is important to God? Are we devoted to our kingdom or God's kingdom?

As I was finishing this chapter, I received a phone call from my brother and listened in shock as he told me my nephew's son was killed in a motorcycle accident late the previous night. He was attending Bible College in California and had a desire to go into the ministry. He was only eighteen years old and had not even finished his first year of college. His time on earth is done, and now he is in the presence of Jesus.

Life is full of reversals, tragedies, disappointments, and separations. Each one of us affected by this loss stands at this bitter or better fork in the road again. We can be angry and bitter at this horrendous loss and wallow in self-pity, or we can believe in a sovereign God who is in control and who will empower us with His Holy Spirit to walk through to the other side. His parents and brothers have chosen to take the better road, and they are glorifying God through this incredibly painful trial. This trial has squeezed them, and the fragrance of Christ is coming out. They know that this separation is just temporary and that all will be made right someday. They are trusting that God's plan is better than theirs, although it sure doesn't feel like it. Corrie Ten Boom once said, "Although the threads of my life have often seemed knotted, I know by faith that on the other side of the embroidery there is a crown."

Everyone has trials, and some people seem to have more than others. The Bible is full of stories that include pain, suffering, and times of testing. We find there are certain characters who had outrageous trials and yet responded in amazing ways with a trust in God's plan and not their own. One of these stories tells how Joseph was betrayed by his brothers and sold into slavery. While faithfully serving his master, he was wrongly accused by a seductive woman and thrown into prison. From a human perspective, these events in Joseph's life do not make any sense. Joseph made good decisions, and then he was punished for what he did right. It is easy to question where God was in so many of his circumstances. Joseph could have easily taken the bitter road, but he chose the better road. God was orchestrating a much bigger picture but had not shared it with Joseph. At the end of Joseph's life, we see how God was fitting all things together for his good and blessing. There was a much bigger purpose unfolding. It's a beautiful picture of forgiveness and salvation for Joseph's entire family. In Genesis, the first book in the Bible, we can read about all that Joseph experienced and his godly response to the trials that came his way.

The most amazing story of all is the story of Jesus. He was born in a dusty barn and into a humble family. The authorities of that day were out to destroy Him from the very beginning. He did everything right and was wrongly accused and suffered greatly. He was sent by God, His Father, to give mankind an amazing gift—eternal life in heaven. He healed the sick, performed miracles, and did good everywhere He went. His disciples knew He was the Messiah, and yet there were others who constantly misunderstood and accused Jesus at every turn. The religious leaders of that day tried to kill Him, but He didn't defend Himself or fight back. He could have annihilated anyone who came against Him, but He didn't. He never once felt sorry for Himself. Jesus knew His purpose on earth was to redeem us back to God—to take on our sins and pay the price for our salvation.

Jesus did not deserve to die, but He allowed Himself to be nailed to the cross for us. He was obedient to His Father's will. His death looked like defeat, but everything changed on the third day after His crucifixion. He arose and came out of that tomb conquering sin and death. This amazing victory over death allows us to take on His righteousness when we repent and accept Jesus as Savior. When we take on His righteousness, we are made right before God. What an amazing gift. Thank God He had a better plan!

> God made Him who had no sin to be sin for us, so
> that in Him we might become the righteousness of
> God. (2 Corinthians 5:21 NIV)

The gospel message is a story of hope. It is the answer to all pain and suffering here. God's gift to us was wrapped in a body that was hanging on a cross, beaten and broken. No wonder the two disciples on the road to Emmaus were discouraged and confused. This did not make any sense to their human minds. All they could see in this seemingly tragic event was defeat. To them, it looked like it was the end of the story until Jesus came alongside and walked with them.

It is so easy to misinterpret things. When life does not go the way we want, we quite often react like the graduate who walked away from his father. We often view God as austere or harsh. It sometimes feels like we are getting hit by a tidal wave and that God does not love us. Although life might feel that way sometimes, God does not change. God is love and is full of compassion and cares for each one of us. Sadly, we are often the ones who invite sin and destruction into our lives by disobedience to God's plan. We choose to live life our way and then want God to fix it when things fall apart. We somehow don't think that the reaping and sowing principle applies to us. Galatians 6:7 (NKJV) says, "Do not be deceived, God is not mocked; for whatever a man sows, that he will also reap." God is holy and hates sin, but He loves the sinner. He never condones sin or evil and does not send it into our lives. Instead, He has offered us forgiveness and a way through to life eternal with Him. Satan would love for us to think differently, and he wants us to put all the blame on God.

Our perspective about God is huge and greatly affects how we live. When we realize that life is not all about us, we will understand we are here on planet Earth to serve God. When we truly get a revelation of how much God loves us and that His view of life is so much different than ours, it will create a paradigm shift in our thinking.

Paradigm shifts can be so life changing. It's like the story of the man who entered the subway in New York one Sunday morning. Those on the subway were enjoying the quiet ride until this father with his loud and rambunctious children got on. He sat down and closed his eyes, oblivious to his children's disruptive behavior. The gentleman sitting next to the children couldn't take it anymore and said to their father, "Sir, your children are really disturbing a lot of people. I wonder if you couldn't control them a little better."

The man opened his eyes and said softly, "Oh, you're right. I guess I should do something about it. We just came from the hospital where their mother died about an hour ago. I don't know what to think, and I guess they don't know how to handle it either."

What a paradigm shift for this man who had just reprimanded the father—what a changed perspective. Instead of irritation, now came sympathy, compassion, and the desire to help. I think the same is true for us in our lives. If we could see things as God sees them, we would agree with Him, have a greater compassion for others, and have a clearer perspective knowing that although we don't see the whole picture, He does.

It has been said that God answers our prayers the way we would want them answered if we had all the facts. I have pondered this for a long time because I've had some terrible disappointments in my life. When a loved one is taken from us, how does this make sense when it feels so bad? I believe when we fully realize that God is sovereign and does all things right, we can have the peace He gives to His dearly loved children in a world that is broken and under the curse of sin. God is omnibenevolent, which simply means He is perfectly good and all-loving.

> For the Lord is good and His love endures forever;
> His faithfulness continues through all generations.
> (Psalm 100:5 NIV)

God wants us to have a right perspective of Him. He is God—the one and only true God. He is our Creator, and He holds our breath and our heartbeat in His hands. God wants for us to know Him personally, and He wants to partner with us through life. He loves each one of us unconditionally. He wants us to live victoriously and have that abundant life He talks about in John 10. He wants us to live above the storms of life, and the only way to do that is by His Holy Spirit living in us. He wants to be our light behind the dark shadows of this life.

John 10:10 (NKJV) tells us: "The thief does not come except to steal, and to kill, and to destroy. I have come that they may have life, and that they may have it more abundantly."

God has plans, not problems for our lives.

—Corrie Ten Boom

The Weaver

by Alt, Tabb, and Tullar

My life is but a weaving
Between my Lord and me;
I cannot choose the colors
He worketh steadily.

Oft times He weaveth sorrow
And I, in foolish pride,
Forget He sees the upper,
And I the underside.

Not til the loom is silent
And the shuttles cease to fly,
Shall God unroll the canvas
And explain the reason why.

The dark threads are as needful
In the Weaver's skillful hand,
As the threads of gold and silver
In the pattern He has planned.

He knows, He loves, He cares,
Nothing this truth can dim.
He gives His very best to those
Who chose to walk with Him.

SECTION 2
STORMY SEAS

Yea though I walk through the valley of the shadow of
death, I will fear no evil, for You are with me.

—Psalm 23:4 (NKJV)

3

"MY SHEEP ARE MORE IMPORTANT THAN YOUR COWS!"

But He knows the way that I take; when He has tested me,
I shall come forth as gold.

—Job 23:10 (NKJV)

It was a warm spring day, and I had been out building fences. We were expecting another shipment of cattle in a few days, so I was scrambling to get the temporary hot wire strung as we planned to rotational graze the herd. It was Friday, May 28, 2010, and it was our twenty-second wedding anniversary. It was an ordinary day filled with normal ranch activities. My husband, Eric, and I had celebrated our anniversary earlier that week with a dinner out at our favorite restaurant. On the actual anniversary night, we decided to go out as a family and take our daughter with us. Our plan was to go to Idaho Falls and try out the new barbecue place and then see a movie. Little did I know that a violent storm cloud was about to burst wide open over my life. I had absolutely no idea that on this night the valley of the shadow of death was coming my way. I had survived some close calls in life and had gone through some difficult trials, but they paled in comparison to the enormous black cloud I was about to enter. I did not know when I left the ranch that night that I would not be returning for nearly a month.

The new restaurant was very busy that evening, so we sat down in the foyer to wait for our table and look through the menu. I was dreaming of a tasty plate of barbecue and looking forward to a fun evening out.

Suddenly, my left foot started to tingle, and it was *intense*. I told Eric, "My foot feels funny, so I think I'll walk it out."

I left the restaurant and walked up and down the sidewalk out in front. As I walked, my foot literally started to buck. I went back in the restaurant and sat down, asking Eric if he could feel my foot. My foot and ankle were now in full spasm.

"Are you doing that?" he asked.

I replied, "No, I have no control of my foot."

His response was, "We need to get that checked."

Normally, I would have panicked, but I truly think my brain was already going into shock. I very calmly agreed, and we got up to leave the restaurant. As we reached the door, I realized I had no feeling in my left leg. I remember thinking that it felt like there was a log attached to my hip and I was simply dragging this dead weight. I said to my daughter, Marti, "Sis, hang onto me. I can't feel my leg."

We made it outside the restaurant, and I slumped down on a big rock beside the door. I do not remember much, but my daughter recalls that my entire leg was bucking and completely out of control. My last words were, "Hang onto my leg! I can't control it!" I then slipped out of consciousness with my eyes wide open in a dead stare.

Marti knew from previous experiences that you do not want a person in distress to lose consciousness, so she grabbed my face and looked me in the eyes and cried, "Mom, stay with me. Help is on the way!" She told me later she thought I had died because there was no life in my eyes. I was staring right through her.

Eric raced out to get our pickup, and by the time he drove up to the front of the restaurant, he found me in a full-blown grand mal seizure. The seizure started in my left foot and worked its way up my leg, and when it hit my torso, I checked out. My family told me later that as people gathered around, one guy shouted out, "Someone call 911." Another gal stooped down and started mouth-to-mouth resuscitation as I lay there quietly without breathing. Within minutes, the ambulance arrived, and I was transported to Eastern Idaho Regional Medical Center (EIRMC).

On the way there, I regained consciousness. There were men working over me and a young girl sitting beside me. It was my daughter, Marti, but I did not know her. The paramedics were asking me random questions, but nothing made sense. I was answering their questions, but Marti said none of my answers were correct. She was quite impressed at my confidence, especially when I gave them my Social Security number. She said it was a wild and random grouping of numbers. Everything was so foggy. I had no pain, but I couldn't think clearly. We arrived at the hospital, and as they slid the stretcher out of the ambulance, I saw Eric. He was waiting right there and reached out and grabbed my hand. I recognized someone!

I asked him what was going on, and he answered, "You had a grand mal seizure." That did not make any sense to me because I had not been sick and wasn't having any symptoms to warn me of the coming storm.

Minutes later, we were in the emergency room, and they were pulling my clothes off. I had wet my pants. *You have got to be kidding me!* I thought. *How incredibly embarrassing. I am fifty years old, and I just wet my pants. This was so not good.* The rest of that night is a dark memory for me. The doctor came in and said there is usually one of three reasons a person has a grand mal seizure: infection, epilepsy, or a mass in the brain. I was wheeled away for a CT scan, which revealed the news that no one wants to hear: "You have a brain tumor."

In a flash, life became very precious to me and to those who loved me. I have to say those five words threw me into a deep, dark place. I was coming out of this very thick mental fog. My brain had just encountered a massive lightning storm with this grand mal seizure. The fog was lifting, and my mind was screaming *Noooo!* The thoughts that followed were gut-wrenching. I wondered if I would survive the surgery or if I was going to die a miserable death. Doris had a brain tumor, and she suffered greatly. She lost the ability to see and speak. I feared that I would not be able to think clearly on the other side of surgery. I was hoping someone would tell me that this was just a very bad dream.

The doctor explained to us the type of tumor I had was a meningioma and was usually very slow growing and likely benign. He said I could have had this tumor for twenty to thirty years. The good news was it was in a good place to operate, but the bad news was it was quite large and needed to be removed. So happy anniversary! I was going to have brain surgery.

The crazy thing was I never had any symptoms that would indicate a brain tumor. I felt great and very rarely had headaches. I had not been drinking enough water that day while fencing, and so the theory was I had become dehydrated, which, in turn, had caused my brain to swell just enough for the tumor to trigger a grand mal seizure.

The next few days were surreal. It was Memorial Day weekend, so putting a surgical team together was not going to happen for a few days. Surgery was scheduled for June 1, 2010. I had three days to look forward to this monumental event. Valium had now become my best friend. I was not looking forward to what lay ahead, and I was not a big fan of MRIs. I have a serious aversion to tight places, and the MRI machine was definitely not invented with those fears in mind. I used to scuba dive, and after having a close call under water, I have never been quite the same in tight spaces. My sister flew in from Seattle and would sit with me through the forty-five minutes of the MRI sessions. She would call out, "You're almost done!" when I had only been in there for five minutes. You've got to love the faithfulness of a devoted sister. The dreaded day of June 1 arrived. I would have my hair shaved off, and following that ordeal, they were going to take power tools to my head! Surgery was scheduled for five o'clock in the evening, but at ten o'clock in the morning, the nurse arrived with hair clippers. My stomach sank. The first chunk of hair hit the sheets, and I wanted to cry. This was really going to happen!

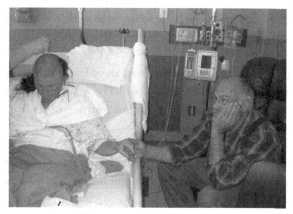

Shaving my head for surgery

After the head shaving came the brain mapping and another one of the dreaded MRIs. Oh, I could think of better ways to spend my day. I was scared! The next few hours were a blur with family and friends coming to visit us. They all stood around my bed and prayed, but I do not remember much.

Then it happened—that dreaded moment when the medical team came and said, "Mrs. Anthony, it's time for surgery."

My husband and daughter escorted me to the surgery area. The smells, the sounds, the hanging tools from the ceiling—it was all too much for my brain, so I asked to be sedated immediately. I kissed them both goodbye and disappeared into an unconscious state for three days.

The six-hour surgery was successful, but I was paralyzed on my left side. I emerged from the intensive care unit three days later, sporting a head turban that was fitted with wound drain tubes. I could think, and

I was able to speak. *Thank You, God!* However, I was shocked to find that my entire left side from the neck down was completely paralyzed. What a helpless feeling to look at my arm and leg and not have any connection. The medical staff would poke my left leg with a needle and ask, "Can you feel that?" but I couldn't. Thankfully, the paralysis was temporary. Feeling came back to my arm within a few days, but it took a few months before my left leg would wake up again.

The pathology report came back several days later with the news that my tumor was benign. *Thank You, Jesus!* The good news was no more treatment was needed, but now the long journey of learning how to walk again was about to begin.

The days in the hospital were filled with physical therapy and learning how to function with this new disability. There was one particular day I remember so clearly when I hit an all-time low. I had just come out of ICU, and the nurses had come to remove my staples, stitches, drain tubes, and turban, and I was then cleared to take a shower. I was lifted into a wheelchair, and my daughter pushed me into the small bathroom in my room. As I sat there naked and broken, I wept as I watched the blood and yellow betadine solution used on my head during surgery drip down onto my legs and then down the drain. Just ten days prior, I had been in jeans and cowboy boots riding my horse and checking cattle on the desert. I was doing what I loved to do and in full control of my body. Now I needed to have someone shower me and help me go to the bathroom. I did not know whether I would ever be able to ride horses again. My life as I knew it had changed forever.

During this same time, just seven days after my surgery, my niece's four-month-old baby boy died of sudden infant death syndrome (SIDS). It was an unbelievable grief for our family, especially to my niece and her husband. To bury a child was a far greater trial than what I was going through. Their lives had also just changed forever. Life for us and our extended family seemed to be spinning out of control.

Life can change for any of us in a matter of seconds. It might be a phone call that changes the course of our lives or an accident that leaves us disabled. It could be the pathology report that is positive for cancer or the sudden death of someone we loved. It is during those times that our perspectives about life and God can drastically change.

The brain tumor surgery was like a tidal wave that swept over me. This storm rolled into my life without warning and flattened me out. God had started a paradigm shift in my life years before, and He was changing my perspective of Himself and life, but now He had my full attention. I was staring straight on at my mortality. Now I was the one going through the storm. Now I was the one who had lost the ability to function normally.

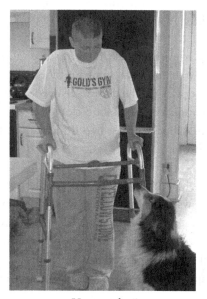

Home at last!

Three weeks after surgery I was released from the hospital. Home had never looked so good. I started therapy on my leg, which required someone to drive the 120-mile round trip with me to Idaho Falls twice a week.

After being home a week, one morning I woke with flu-like symptoms. My leg looked kind of swollen with a darker color, and I felt nauseated and chilled. We headed to physical therapy, and I got on the exercise bike and pedaled with my good leg (training my paralyzed leg) for forty-five minutes. On the way home, we decided to stop by the emergency room to make sure all was well because I was feeling pretty uncomfortable. The ER doctor took one look at my leg and ordered an ultrasound. I had a deep vein thrombosis (DVT) from my hip to my knee. Because my leg was still numb, I had no pain, so the only symptom I was aware of was the swelling and color change in my leg.

The doctor came in and told me, "You are one lucky lady!" He went on to tell me if the clot had broken free, it would have been instant death. I knew this was not because I was lucky but rather God controlling the details of my life.

I was immediately admitted back into the hospital, only this time to the cardiology department. I was put on blood thinners and had an IV put in to slow down my heart rate if needed. It was a very long night, as the fear of breaking the blood clot loose was constantly in my thoughts. Once the blood thinner had done its job, I was once again released from the hospital.

My journey continued with many bumps in the road, but after about four months, I was walking again, first with a walker and then with a cane. I still have some paralysis in my left leg and have a bit of a limp, but I will take it. I am so thankful to be mobile again, and I have a new appreciation for all the things I used to take for granted. I am so grateful I can walk, pick up a cup of coffee, and take a shower on my own.

As I look back over all of the events surrounding this storm in my life, I clearly see God's divine plan and hand in my life. He truly is the light behind all the shadows. He was carrying me through and orchestrating all the details. That near-fatal night we chose to go to Idaho Falls instead of Pocatello, allowing us to be right near EIRMC, the closest trauma center hospital with an excellent neurological staff. The restaurant we chose was right near the main fire station, so the emergency medical team was there in about four minutes. Why we celebrated our anniversary early will remain a mystery, but for some reason we did that year, so our daughter was with us the night this storm hit my life with full force. Another giant blessing was the army of friends who came forward to help with the ranch and all our needs at home. God provided for us miraculously during those times. So many people came alongside us and brought food, gave us money, and helped with all our animals. These people were willing to be God's hands and feet. We were humbled!

I shudder to think about the week before my grand mal seizure. I had been riding a young horse out on the desert by myself to check cattle. If my leg had gone into spasms on a green colt, I can only imagine the reaction the horse would have had. Then how long would it have been before anyone found me? I most likely would have died without help. God's hand was truly on me, and everything was in His control, although at times it felt like the waves of trial and testing were crashing over me.

This storm hit me hard physically, but it also hit us hard financially. We are self-employed, so all the time off was costly. My husband has his own mobile diesel repair business, which is our main source of income, and my daughter and I run the ranch. Just four years earlier, we had suffered from a cattle fraud business transaction, which left us nearly bankrupt. We lost thousands of dollars from this deal, and in order to make our annual land payments, vet bills, and other expenses that year, we were forced to sell a hundred acres of hay ground. We also canceled our medical health insurance policy. We were just trying to survive. The spring of my brain tumor surgery we had just been talking about renewing our policy, but before we were able to renew, I had a grand mal seizure. Now not only was I crippled physically, but we were crippled financially as well. Brain surgery is *expensive.*

41

Six months prior to my brain tumor surgery, I had been listening to some ministry teaching on the fact that we are not able or responsible to change others, but we can change ourselves. We were struggling in our marriage, in our finances, with the ranch, and with many other things, and I was tired of it. So with this new view of taking responsibility for me, I wrote down some specific goals and then prayed, "Lord, change me!" I had no idea at the time just how God was going to do that.

During the spring, just before this trial hit, I was very busy with ranch work and with a new business adventure that I was working on. I was invited to attend a leadership conference in Anaheim, California, for this new business venture, but because funds were tight, I really debated whether I should go. A kind friend gave me money for the trip, and my sister blessed me with a free airline pass, so in the middle of April, I was bound for California. On the way home from the conference, I sat next to an elderly lady on the plane who was involved with a prayer ministry. She asked if she could pray with me about my new business adventure. I said that would be great, so right there on the plane, she started to pray for me. Halfway through the prayer, she stopped and said, "Colleen, I sense that God is going to do something very big in your life."

She now had my attention. I was thinking monetary success and big bucks. She continued to pray and then stopped again, "Colleen, I sense this is going to be very soon, and you better hang on!"

I was now very excited as I imagined big boats and ranch expansion. The earlier prayer, "Lord, change me," had left my thoughts. Instead, I envisioned debt-free living and financial independence. She handed me her business card when we landed, and we parted ways. It was just about a month later when I had my grand mal seizure, and life for me changed in a mighty way.

Interestingly enough, I was never was able to reconnect with this lady. Several months after my surgery, I recalled our prayer time on the airplane. I dug out her business card and tried to make contact. There was no answer to my calls and no response to my emails. I believe God orchestrated this divine appointment before the storm to show me that He was in control.

During the months following my surgery, I spent hours on the couch at home trying to learn how to use my left side again. Being an A-type personality with a tremendous amount of drive, this was a new thing for me. I was always on the move, making things happen. Now I was confined to the couch and dependent on others to help me. This is a very hard thing for someone who is as active, driven, and independent as I am.

This down time gave me plenty of opportunity to read, pray, and reflect. I recalled that I had invited God to make some changes in my life. Thankfully, I was never angry at Him during this storm but rather very thoughtful and thankful to be alive. I knew that He was working in my life to bring about change—lots of change. I do not for a minute feel like God sent this brain tumor to change me, but He used a near-tragic life event to refine me.

Some of the changes in my life have been physical, but most of the changes have been spiritual. He used the physical to get to the spiritual. He has changed my perspective of Him. I have felt His love and His care for me through those difficult and terrifying days. He was there and held my hand. He carried me through and showed me how powerful it is to have Him be in charge.

I sensed in my spirit that God was clearly giving me a message: His sheep are more important than my cows. So many times in scripture we read about God's people referred to as sheep. Jesus says, "I am the good Shepherd. The good Shepherd gives His life for the sheep" (John 10:11 NKJV). The Lord was telling me that I had a wrong focus in life. My priority was to build up the cattle operation and keep buying more and more. Building up the ranch was not wrong, but my emphasis on it was. People (God's sheep) are far more valuable than livestock. God was telling me to shift my focus—to love people, even the unlovely ones. It is so easy in life to get caught up in the things we want to do. We put our focus on what we think will make us happy. As a follower of Jesus, my focus should be on what is important to Him. His sheep are very important to Him!

Sometimes it takes almost losing your life to realize just how precious it is. Life is fragile and can change very quickly. Life is also very short and should be lived intentionally. The thought that kept coming to my mind was, *What if I had died during this ordeal?* I knew that if I had died, I would have gone to be with Jesus, but what would He say to me about the fifty years I had spent on planet Earth? How many people were affected in a positive way by my existence? Was I spending my time for me or for Him? If I answered this question honestly, I was horrified to realize that my life was all about me and what I wanted to accomplish.

My brain tumor trial has changed me forever. My focus on what matters the most has changed greatly. I have started to realize just how fragile life is and how important people are to God. Life is so very brief, and the things that we think will make us happy are not what true happiness is about. True joy comes in knowing God and knowing with confidence that we are going to spend eternity with Him.

> When you are dying—when you stand at the gate of eternity—you see things from a different perspective than when you think you may live for a long time. (Corrie Ten Boom)

So often in life, our trials bring blessings where we do not expect them. It is in the dark storms of life that we see God in new and wonderful ways. This *thorn* of brain surgery allowed me to experience God's presence in ways I have never experienced before. Would I want to go through this again? Not in a million years. However, I am thankful to God for the changes He has brought about in my life. He is not only my Savior and Lord, but He is truly my friend. Out of this dark storm came a huge paradigm shift for me. I, like Doris, could now say in the flames of a trial: God is so good! He truly is the light behind the shadows on this sometimes very dark sea of life.

God gave me this poem during my recovery time, and it deeply touched my heart.

The Thorn

by Martha Snell Nicholson

I stood, a mendicant of God, before His royal throne
and begged Him for one priceless gift, which I could
call my own.
I took the gift from out His hand, but as I would
depart I cried,
"But Lord, this is a thorn and it has pierced my heart.
This is a strange and hurtful gift which Thou hast
given me."
He said, "My child, I give good gifts. I gave My best
to thee."
I took it home. And though at first the cruel thorn
hurt sore,
as long years passed I learned at last to love it more
and more.
I learned He never gives a thorn without this added
grace:
He takes the thorn to pin aside the veil which hides
His face.

"For My thoughts are not your thoughts, nor are
your ways my ways," says the Lord.
—Isaiah 55:8 (NKJV)

"GET IN THE BOAT!"

When He [Jesus] had finished speaking, He said to Simon [Peter],
"Put out into the deep water, and let down the nets for a catch."

—Luke 5:4 (NIV)

My dad use to say, "Cheer up! Things could get worse. So I cheered up,
and sure enough, they did." We would laugh every time he joked about
this, but sometimes in life it seems so true. This is how I felt when I
was diagnosed with breast cancer.

During the summer of 2013, life had almost resumed to a normal
pace after my brain surgery. I still had a limp and my foot and ankle
were still weak with some numbness, but I had learned to navigate
around my limitations. Our daughter had decided to attend a short-
term mission trip to Russia with our church, so I was doing all the
ranch chores during those two weeks while she was away.

It was the middle of July, and we were irrigating pastures and doing
basic chores around the farm. I was having quite a bit of shoulder pain
at that time, so I opted to have a deep-tissue massage. The gal who was
performing the massage was so aggressive that she bruised my shoulder
area. I was supposed to drink a lot of water following the massage but
had not, and I felt sick. Two days later while showering, I discovered a
very large lump in my left breast. It was so large that you could almost
see it. I freaked out and went into complete panic mode. How could
this be? I had just been to the doctor in February, and everything was
fine. After much discussion with my medical team, the conclusion was

47

that tumors do not usually appear that fast and it was probably just a swollen lymph gland from all the toxins released by the deep-tissue massage.

My doctor said, "Let's just keep an eye on it, and if it does not go away in a few months, then we will take a closer look."

The swelling went down but there was still a small lump. From the end of July to the following January, I went into serious prayer mode asking God to take the lump away. January 2014 rolled around, and the lump was still there. I made another doctor's appointment, and this time the advice was I should get a mammogram and ultrasound. I scheduled an appointment for January 13, 2014, and the verse I read that morning in my devotional time was Isaiah 41:10 (NLT): "Don't be afraid for I am with you. Don't be discouraged, for I am your God. I will strengthen you and help you. I will hold you with My victorious right hand."

I had peace regarding this visit, and all went smoothly. After the ultrasound, I consulted with the doctor. He said the lump had some good features and some bad features, so he was ordering a biopsy. Yikes! I did not like the look on my doctor's face and knew in my heart that something was wrong. The biopsy procedure was scheduled for January 24. I hated that I had to go through all these medical procedures all over again, but the morning of my biopsy, I got some encouragement from a devotional titled *Stay Calm*. It was about the children of Israel being pursued by the Egyptians as they were about to cross through the Red Sea. The verse was, Exodus 14:13–14 (NKJV): "Do not be afraid. Stand still, and see the salvation of the Lord which He will accomplish for you today … The Lord will fight for you." It seemed to me that I was getting a consistent message from God. I was not to fear or be discouraged but to stand still (or be quiet and settled), and I would see His deliverance. He was going to fight this battle. Now I had to grab onto that and believe it.

The biopsy procedure went amazingly well. I had been dreading it, but the day came and I had tremendous peace. I knew that God was with me. Actually, during the procedure, I sensed His presence like never before. I had that peace that surpasses all understanding that is mentioned in Philippians 4:7. Once the biopsy was completed, I had to patiently wait for the pathology results. The day before I was to receive my report, I prayed and fasted. I felt strongly that I needed to spend time with God in prayer.

The message I got during that time of prayer was to *trust God through the hard times.* "Yea, though I walk through the valley of the shadow of death, I will fear no evil, for You are with me" (Psalm 23:4 NKJV). I sensed that God was preparing me to *go through.* I did not know what the *through* part actually meant, but I did not like the timing of this message. I was hoping this message was for the scary tests I had just gone through and not something that was coming up.

However, my hopes were dashed when the biopsy revealed cancer in all seven cores. As I sat in the exam room and heard those words, "You have breast cancer," my mouth went dry and my hands turned ice cold. God's answer to my prayer was not what I wanted to hear. My thought was, *You mean my brain tumor and blood clot and everything else I've been through was not enough?* God had more changes to make to my character and paradigm.

I was being squeezed again, and that old false paradigm was showing up. I started to question God's ways. I questioned His love for me. Had I done something wrong that I was being punished for? Sadly, my focus was inward, and I was not seeing any good in this scary diagnosis. This seemed like an odd way for God to show me that He was good.

I turned to the Lord in prayer and fell on my face again, asking Him for direction through this fog. I felt numb and withdrew into a quiet place down deep in my soul. I spent hours reviewing my fasting notes and reading my Bible seeking answers as to why this dark cloud had enveloped me. Was this trial for refinement in my life to produce more fruit for Him? Was I being disciplined? Or was this just life happening to me? I know that God does not send grief into our lives, but He can allow it. I believe when we belong to Him, everything that comes at us has to be reviewed by Him first. He can heal us, He can prevent things from coming at us, or He can say, "This is for your good and blessing and My bigger plan." He has promised that He will never abandon us.

> For He Himself has said, "I will never leave you nor forsake you." So we may boldly say: "The Lord is my helper; I will not fear. What can man do to me?" (Hebrews 13:5–6 NKJV)

I know with all my heart that God is omniscient. He knows everything from the beginning to the end. He created me and gave me life. I was earnestly seeking His face and desiring answers as to why another dark cloud had entered my life. I have learned that sometimes we do not get exact or immediate answers and His response is to just trust Him.

The message God gave me was profound in so many ways. I was going to *go through*, and I would come through victorious. God was looking for my heart to surrender like Esther's was "for such a time as this" (Esther 4:14 NKJV). God wants to use us for His work down here on earth, but He needs people who are surrendered and who will trust Him. The only way to know if we trust Him is to be tested. I was being tested—*again*. Surgery was scheduled for January 31. The day of surgery, I got up to spend time with God. We had to be at the hospital early, so I found myself in my prayer room around four o'clock in the morning. God was giving me supernatural peace. I was not looking forward to the day, but I was not afraid. The doctors were still undecided as to whether to perform a lumpectomy, a mastectomy, or a double mastectomy. It was still unknown if the cancer had spread to any of my lymph nodes. I had told the surgeon to remove whatever was necessary, and I asked God to go before me and fight this battle.

My daily Bible reading that morning was the same message I had been getting over and over, only this time not from a devotional book but from where I was at in my daily reading of the Bible. It was the same verse in Exodus: "Do not be afraid. Stand still, and see the salvation of the Lord which He will accomplish for you today. For the Egyptians whom you see today, you shall see again no more forever. The Lord will fight for you and you shall hold your peace" (Exodus 14:13–14 NKJV).

Even though this is an Old Testament story, God was encouraging me with the message that He was going to see me through, just like He did for the children of Israel. He is the same God today, and He can still part the Red Sea and get His children through a difficulty. He is still a miracle-working God. The message to me was that I would *go through* this trial and that God would wipe out the enemy that was pursuing me. To me, this was a message that surgery would be successful, and every single cancer cell would be eliminated. Three times over I had received this message from different sources. I had an overwhelming sense of peace and felt confident that God was with me.

The surgery went well (other than a few very painful procedures), and the surgeon was able to remove the tumor by performing a lumpectomy. Thank You, Lord!

On February 3, I met with my surgeon to get the pathology news. The verses I received that morning during my devotions were once again the same message about the children of Israel fleeing from the enemy and how God had fought for them and how He had delivered them. The verse that stood out to me that morning was Exodus 14:28 (NLT): "Of all the Egyptians who had chased the Israelites into the sea, not a single one survived." My prayer was that God had slain all my enemies and not one cancer cell remained!

My pathology report showed that it was the common type of breast cancer and that they had clean margins all around the tumor removal. They took six lymph nodes, and only one was cancerous. My oncology team felt confident they had removed it all. Praise God! However, because the cancer was in one lymph node, chemo and radiation were both recommended.

I have watched many people die from cancer, and I am not a fan of chemotherapy. I had seen what chemo did to my sister-in-law who had died from ovarian cancer, and I was positive that I did not want to sign up for this. I consulted with my oncologist, and he made his recommendations of a full-blown treatment plan, which, by law, he was required to do. I then asked him what he would do if this was his wife. He smiled and said he would probably order an oncotype DX test, which predicts how likely the cancer is to return after surgery. The scale for this test, as I understand it, is 1–100, but normally, the numbers would fall between 7 and 45. The lower the number is on this test, the better. My oncologist explained to me that if my number was in the low range, then I would probably be safe to not do chemo. If it came back in the midrange, then we should really discuss chemo. However, if my number was in the high range, which at that time was anything higher than 18, then he would highly recommend that I go through chemo and radiation.

This onco test was expensive, but we felt it was worth doing. I started to pray for my number to be 7, which was what my oncologist said was the lowest they had seen to date. I figured this would be a good sign that chemo was not needed. I really valued my doctor's opinion on treatment, but I did not want chemo unless I absolutely needed it. I did not want to take any chances with my health, but I also didn't want to destroy my body with chemo. I was looking for confirmation on what I believed God was saying to me about what to do. The *going through* part was what I was struggling with. Had I already *gone through*, or was God telling me *to go through all treatment*?

My oncologist called on a Thursday and said, "Well, you're out of the gray area. Your test results are at 27. I have ordered your chemo to start next Tuesday."

I was devastated!

The surgeon felt confident they had removed everything, but the oncology team said it only takes one cell to spread, and with my type of cancer being so aggressive, I should not risk it. If my cancer returned, it would most likely go to my bones, and I would be in the fight of my life. The doctor explained that the chemo would kill anything they missed in my lymph system, and radiation would get anything at the tumor site. The five-year plan of taking the estrogen blocker medicine would follow after chemo and radiation and would starve out anything else. I knew the doctor was adamant about playing it safe, but I had seen firsthand what chemo does to people. Sometimes the treatment is worse than the disease. I felt like God was telling me to trust Him; this was His fight, and He was going to wipe out my enemy. I was really struggling with the *going through* part.

Not knowing for sure what to do, I again went back to the only one who does know and asked God through prayer and fasting what I should do. My prayer was that because I felt like God had told me that *the entire enemy was eliminated*, why should I do chemo and radiation and jeopardize my immune system? I did not want to *go through* that part of the trial.

I know that God can heal in many different ways. He can just speak a word and heal miraculously, or He can direct us to go through treatment. I also know that sometimes He chooses to just heal us by taking us home to heaven if He decides our time here on planet Earth is done. I wanted to be healed and needed God to tell me what to do.

Years ago, I had started the habit of praying and fasting and seeking God's face. During those times, I would journal throughout the day. I would write down things that I had read out of the Bible or devotional books, as well as things that I heard on Christian radio or ministry recordings. At the end of the fast, I would go back through my journals and summarize my notes. Nearly every time I have done this, there has been a very clear message for me, and I find it reiterated three or four times over from different sources.

I began to seek God's advice about what to do regarding my breast cancer treatment plan. The message that came that day about what to do was this: "Sometimes God asks you to do things that don't make sense in our human thinking."

The first story God gave me was about Naaman (2 Kings 5) the leper, who came to the man of God named Elisha and asked to be healed. Elisha sent word to him to go dip in the Jordan River seven times, and he would be healed. Naaman went away angry and said, "Behold, I thought he would surely come out to me and stand and call on the name of the Lord his God, and strike his hand over the place and recover the leper. Are not Abana and Pharpar, the rivers of Damascus better than all the waters of Israel? May I not wash in them and be clean? So he turned and went away in a rage" (2 Kings 5:11–12 KJV).

Naaman did not like God's answer. First, he wanted an instant healing, and second, if he had to go through treatment, why a dirty river like the Jordan? It did not make sense to put his open leprous wounds in dirty water. Wow, could I ever relate! I was hoping God would just heal me. I too wanted that instant healing. God was testing Naaman's faith and obedience. Naaman finally did obey and dipped in the Jordan seven times like he was told to do, and he was completely healed.

The second message I got from God during that day of prayer and fasting was about Peter who had been fishing all night (Luke 5). He was mending his nets after this long night of fishing when Jesus asked to borrow his boat to preach from. When Jesus was done preaching, He told Peter, "Now go out where it is deeper, and let down your nets to catch some fish" (Luke 5:4 NLT).

To Peter, the professional fisherman, it just did not make sense to fish in the daytime. He fished at night when the water temperature was cooler and the fish came up to feed. Besides this, they had just come in from fishing and had caught nothing. In his mind Jesus was a carpenter and a teacher, not a fisherman. Peter had not made the connection yet that this was the Messiah, God's son. Peter was the fisherman, and he knew how to fish.

Peter responded, "Master, we have toiled all night and caught nothing; nevertheless at Your word I will let down the net" (Luke 5:5 NKJV). The story goes on to say, "And when they had done this they caught a great number of fish" (Luke 5:6 NKJV). There were so many fish their boats began to sink.

Luke 5:8 says, "When Simon Peter saw this he fell down at Jesus' knees, saying depart from me, for I am a sinful man, O Lord." Peter obeyed, and huge blessing followed. He went from calling Jesus, *Master* to *Lord*. It was a turning point in Peter's life. Peter and the others with him left everything and became Jesus's disciples (Luke 5:11). They were now becoming fishers of men. This was a giant paradigm shift for Peter.

After this emotional day of praying and seeking God's guidance, the message was clear, though I did not like it. I was sensing that God said to accept the treatment that the doctors had ordered even though the chemo could have some nasty side effects. I needed to trust God and be obedient to His leading. I felt like He was saying, "Trust Me with your immune system, and get in the boat. Push out into the deep, and trust Me with the outcome."

It was a struggle of my will versus God's will. I know God created me. He is the one who has given me life. He holds my heartbeat in His hand. Why do I find it so hard to trust Him and His plan? Why was I finding it hard to trust the Man who died for me? If I cannot trust Him, then who can I trust? I questioned whether these messages were really from Him. I questioned *everything*.

When the mail came that day, there was a large manila envelope from the cancer center. It was my cancer packet, and just looking at this envelope made me sick to my stomach. I knew the information inside would be tough to read, so I took some time to pray over it before I opened it up. I finally had the courage to tackle the information and read that one of the possible side effects of one of the chemotherapy drugs they were planning to give me was leukemia. Are you kidding me?! That is not a side effect but rather a whole new disease! It was too much for my brain to process.

After a long and stressful evening of reading, praying, and studying my notes taken while fasting, I went to bed around three o'clock in the morning but was unable to sleep much. The next morning I returned to my study and analyzed the messages that I felt God had given me during the previous day of prayer and fasting. The message once again was very clear, but I didn't like it and hoped I had misinterpreted it. My pastor called that morning and encouraged me with some verses in Job. He said he felt like I was being prepared to *go through*.

Wow, there it was again, I thought. The verses he read to me were from Job 5:18-19 (NIV): "For He wounds, but He also binds up; He injures, but His hands also heal. From six calamities He will rescue you; in seven no harm will touch you."

I had asked God for an onco number of 7, but my results were a 27. It was again my vending machine approach to prayer. I had pushed the 7 button but got 27 instead. The final decision for me came when my cousin called and said, "Colleen, it's like you're standing on a cliff, and God says, 'Jump, and trust Me to catch you.' But you're saying, 'No, I am too scared!'"

I heard a sermon several years ago about making decisions and the example was used of a ship entering the harbor at night. There were three buoy lights that needed to line up. When all three lights were lined up and had become one, the captain of the ship knew he was on a safe course to enter the harbor. The speaker explained that there are three lights in our lives that need to line up when we make important decisions. These lights are: what the word of God says, what godly council recommends, and what your circumstances indicate. When all three of these lights line up, you are on a safe course.

For me, the first light was I felt like God had told me clearly that I was to *go through*. The second light was the godly council from my pastor when he called and said he felt like I was being prepared to *go through*. The third light was my medical team who were advising full treatment and the fact that my onco number was 27, putting my cancer risk in the red zone. All three lights had lined up, and the message was clear.

I knew deep down in my heart that God was saying, "Get in the boat, and trust Me." He had more lessons to teach me and more miracles to perform for me. God wanted to show me that He was trustworthy and in control. He wanted me to trust Him and surrender to His plan. There were going to be big waves ahead on this stormy sea that He would handle and show Himself to be God.

I was being led to experience a deeper relationship with God. My response to this was, "I would rather read this in a book and learn it that way." However, we do not always learn the lessons as well as we do when we walk through them. There is nothing like experience to be the master teacher. Boot camp will prepare soldiers for war, but the actual battle is where warriors are made.

> The Lord gets His best soldiers out of the highlands of affliction. (Charles Spurgeon)

> God never uses anyone greatly until He tests them deeply. (A. W. Tozer)

After wrestling with God, I came to my decision. I decided to trust God and get in the boat. Chemotherapy and radiation were in my future. I have heard it said I would rather cast my lot with God whom I don't always understand but has all power than with man whom I might understand but has no power.

When I made this decision to do it God's way, I was flooded with an overwhelming sense of peace. I dreaded treatment, but I resolved to go forward with Him. I knew God had something to teach me out in the deep waters of this storm. Sometimes He calms the storm, while other times He calms us in the storm.

My breast cancer treatment began in April 2014. After the surgery and time of healing, I started chemotherapy. I had twelve weeks of chemo followed by six weeks of radiation. I prayed over every bag of chemo, shot, pill, and round of radiation. By the third week of chemo, my hair started falling out in chunks, so I had my sister shave my head. I was once again bald.

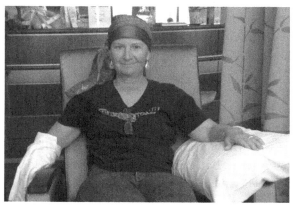

Chemo day

Being bald makes you look sicker than you are. This second time of hair loss for me was harder than the first time. I think the reason was because I was so much more aware this time, and I would be bald for longer. With the brain tumor surgery, I was in shock and heavily sedated. Four hours after losing my hair, I was knocked out for surgery, and then I don't remember anything until about three days later when

I came out of ICU. My head was also wrapped in a turban, and by the time it was removed, my hair had already started to grow back.

This breast cancer journey was a different story. I would be wearing a hat or scarf for months. I gave God my bald head and said, "Lord, I give you my baldness; use it for Your kingdom." There would be times in a grocery store or in some public place when someone would touch my arm and ask, "What are you fighting?"

Visiting my mama after treatment

There were many blessings and lessons along the way. So many times I saw God's hand in the little details. He was there helping me through. It was during this time that God gave me this book project, as I mentioned in the foreword. He brought people along who were fighting their own battles of cancer, and we would pray for each other. He gave me a compassionate heart for those going through chemo and radiation or any medical trial, for that matter. It is a sobering event to spend time in a cancer center and is a very clear picture of just how brief life is. God showed me again through this medical journey that His sheep are so much more important than my cattle.

So many people came alongside us during those days. Our dear friends from church offered us one of their cars to use while traveling back and forth for treatment. The car got great gas mileage compared to our old pickup and was a welcomed blessing because we had about a fifty-mile drive each way to the cancer center, and I was going to have radiation treatments every day for six weeks.

One of the little things that God showed me was to be "thankful for the fleas." I had read the story of Corrie Ten Boom in a Nazi prison camp where she and her sister, Betsy, had been put in a barracks that was infested with fleas. Betsy had said to Corrie that they must be thankful for the fleas. Corrie replied that there was no way she could be thankful for the fleas. Betsy responded, "The Lord says to be thankful *in* everything ... not necessarily *for* everything." A few weeks later, they overheard in the prison yard that the guards left their cell alone because of the fleas, and they were able to have their Bible studies without the fear of being caught or harassed.

I had just been reminded of this story when we received our friends' car to use. It was an older car that had been sitting out by the barn and had not been used for a while, and the mice had moved in. It was a wonderful car and so very thoughtful of them to offer it to us. However, I do not like mice. When I was a little girl, I reached into a big fifty-five-gallon grain barrel to scoop out some grain for my horse, and a mouse ran up my arm and onto my face. I have never been the same and have not fully recovered from that scare. When I saw all the mouse droppings in the front seat, I wondered what it would be like to go off the freeway into the ditch at eighty miles per hour. I knew that if one of those mice ran up my pant leg while driving to town, I would come unglued!

The first day came to take the mouse-mobile to town, and I had plans to hit the car wash after treatment. Thankfully, no mice appeared that first trip, and I was trying so hard to be "thankful in the mice, not for the mice." I went to the cancer center and had my radiation treatment and then headed for the car wash. I was parked by the vacuums and was planning to give the interior and trunk a good cleaning. I got out of the car and decided to take my sweatshirt off because it was so warm.

I was wearing a silk cowboy scarf to cover my bald head and did not want to pull it off in the process. I had the sweatshirt over my face as I was carefully holding onto my scarf when I heard a voice say, "Ma'am, I need to write on your window. Is that okay?" I peered out through the hood. She continued to say, "The man who just entered the wash has paid for your car wash."

I looked up and did not recognize him. I have no idea who the man was, but he was God's hands and feet that day in my life. The car wash was only ten dollars and I could have afforded it, but it blessed me so much to know that God cared about the little details of this journey. He was there helping me with the mouse-mobile. I finished vacuuming with a song in my heart. I never did see a mouse. The Creator controls! I'm guessing they had strict orders to stay under the seat. Thank You, God, for washing my car, and thank you to the man who was God's instrument that day. I hope he was blessed in a mighty way.

During my radiation treatments, I would get new x-rays every week. Tuesdays were usually those days. It was extremely difficult to have my arms above my head and hold perfectly still on a metal table for twenty to thirty minutes. The pain from an old shoulder injury was excruciating for me. I dreaded those days. I would quite often meet a friend for breakfast afterward to help calm my nerves. One particular Tuesday was especially rough. After a painful x-ray session, followed by my radiation treatment, I went out to get in the mouse-mobile and discovered that I had a flat tire. Normally, that would not be a big deal, but after going through what I just had gone through, it became a big deal. I got in the car, put my head on the steering wheel, and wept. Sometimes life seems bigger than it really is. I limped over to the gas station about a mile away and dug around for some quarters to put in the air compressor. I was able to get enough air in the tire to drive to the restaurant where my friend was waiting. God had a friend there to pray with me and then escort me to the tire shop. She stayed with me while I waited for the repair. God was in the details of every day and was carrying me through.

Sometimes God asks us to do things that do not make sense to us. I remember hearing a story about this guy who felt led by God to preach the gospel at this lumber camp. He showed up to preach, and every single person left. As he stood there alone, he noticed a monkey in the tree. He sensed in his spirit that God was prompting him to preach anyway, even though it was just him and the monkey. He felt pretty silly preaching to the monkey, and he was very discouraged. However, several years later a man approached him and said he had been at the lumber camp. The day he preached this man had left with all the others but then decided to come back and hid in the wood pile. That day he heard the gospel message and accepted the Lord as his Savior, and it had radically changed his life. He was delighted to see this preacher again and was able to thank him. Had this preacher not obeyed God, he would have missed this amazing blessing. What a lesson to learn. We need to always trust God even if sometimes it doesn't make sense.

Sick from chemo but needed a bit of that desert air

I would rather not repeat the year 2014, but I am thankful for the many blessings and lessons that God showed me along the way. I was ever so thankful for that last day of treatment. God has been with me every step of the way, and I am so thankful for His provision, His mercy, and His grace. He, once again, was my light behind the shadows.

Trust in the Lord with all your heart, and lean
not on your own understanding; In all your ways
acknowledge Him, and He shall direct your paths.

—Proverbs 3:5–6 (NKJV)

"Get into the boat!" Thou didst whisper.
At first how I feared to obey;
I looked not at Thee, but the storm clouds,
The darkness, the waves, and the spray.

But then came the words, "Will you trust Him?
Will you claim and receive at His hand
All His definite fullness of blessing?
Launch out at thy Master's command!"

Thou art willing, my Lord, could I doubt Thee?
Hast Thou ever proved untrue?
Nay! Out at Thy word I have ventured,
I have trusted. Thy part is to do.

by Laura A. Barter-Snow

TSUNAMI

Be still, and know that I am God.

—Psalm 46:10 (NKJV)

We were the Three Musketeers and the best of friends. I have two sisters whom I consider to be my soul mates. There are so many people who don't get along with their families, but our family loves each other deeply and shares a close relationship.

I was about to encounter another storm in life, and it hit with tsunami force. God showed me through my brain tumor that my priorities were wrong, and in the breast cancer journey, He taught me about trusting Him. Now God was about to teach me that He is sovereign.

In 2015 my oldest sister Lynn was diagnosed with a rare form of leukemia. Our family was devastated, but I was confident that God was going to heal her. This disease was nothing to the God who had created her. With a word or a touch, He could raise her up to full health again. The two-year battle was filled with trips to Salt Lake City hospitals and the MD Anderson Cancer Center in Houston for chemotherapy and bone marrow biopsies.

Lynn was one of the most hilarious people I have ever known. She had an amazing sense of humor and was a blast to hang out with. My sister was a woman full of life and passion. She generously gave of her time and money, always investing in the broken and hurting. Lynn was a comforter and encourager to many. She was a woman of faith and a prayer warrior. Lynn had three beautiful girls, eleven grandchildren, and three great-grandchildren. She was also my neighbor, and we talked nearly every day. She was one of my best friends, and I loved her dearly.

I spent many hours in prayer and fasting regarding her illness and had sensed in my spirit that the Lord was saying to me, "Thank Me for her healing." I *was* thanking Him and very confident that even in the eleventh hour He would heal her.

During the fall of 2017, she started to develop more symptoms, and the disease started to raise its ugly head again. The current treatment was no longer effective, so her specialist at MD Anderson ordered her to stop the medication and said they would see her in a month.

I had just received the final print of the book cover from my cousin Josh and had shared it with Lynn in a text message. A few days after sharing the picture with her, I noticed that she had made it her phone screen saver. She said, "Sis, I know that God painted this picture for your book, but He has painted it for me as well. When I can't sleep at night, I just stare at this picture. It's Jesus and me in this storm of cancer. He is with me in the boat."

During that last month, Lynn's condition continued to decline rapidly. The day she flew to Houston for her checkup and new treatment protocol, we drove the three-hour trip from home to the Salt Lake City airport to see them off.

She was feeling the nasty effects of her cancer, and while we were waiting for their flight, she looked at me and said, "Oh sis, what if I come home and I'm healed!"

I responded "Honey, I'm counting on it!"

We were both praying and believing for a miracle from God. I had no idea that this would be our last day together.

They had scheduled return flights for later in the week, and we all thought it was just going to be a routine checkup and a change in her treatment plan. There was also some talk about doing a stem cell transplant because an excellent donor match had been located. My last vivid memory of my precious sister was watching my brother-in-law push her wheelchair down the Jetway onto the plane. She had lost a lot of weight and looked so small sitting there. I had a lump in my throat the size of Texas, but I was holding fast to the message that I believe God had given me: to thank Him for her healing.

They arrived in Houston Sunday evening where they met up with their oldest daughter who had flown in from San Jose. Lynn was in terrible shape by then, and on Monday, they tried to move her appointment up but were unsuccessful. Her appointment was scheduled for Tuesday morning, December 5.

I texted her early that morning and said: "Praying for you today sissie. I know that God has gone before and will see you through. Fear not ... nor be dismayed! He is with you!! Love you so much!"

She responded: "Thank you sis. I needed that. We are enroute to MD. I keep saying God You are fighting this battle."

I sent a text back saying: "Yes He is fighting this battle and we thank Him for your complete healing. He is moving and working even though we don't see it ... it is happening. The waves are big but we will make it to the other side!! He is in the boat with us! You will not sink ... He has you by the hand."

She responded: "and I'm clinging to that." That was the last text I received from my precious sister.

I sent two more messages without any response. I shared with her two verses that, as I read back through months later, I realized were prophetic. They were verses that God had for both of us.

And He said unto her, Daughter, thy faith hath made thee whole; go in peace, and be whole of thy plague. (Mark 5:34 KJV)

And He arose, and rebuked the wind, and said unto the sea, Peace, be still. And the wind ceased, and there was a great calm. (Mark 4:39 KJV)

When my sister arrived at her appointment early that Tuesday morning, they soon realized that her blood pressure and overall condition were very serious. She was immediately sent to the emergency room at MD Anderson where she was later admitted to the intensive care unit. God had other plans for Lynn, and her journey on earth was coming to a close.

Her condition had turned into a very serious case of internal infection, and she was going into septic shock. In the early hours of the following morning, Lynn was having problems breathing, so she was sedated and intubated. We were all tracking her progress, and when things looked serious, we all booked flights to join them in Houston. My other two siblings and Lynn's two other daughters were coming from different locations. We all landed in Houston within a half hour of each other on Wednesday evening, but sadly, we were a couple hours too late. My beloved sister, who was only sixty-seven years old, went home to be with Jesus before we could see her again. When I received the phone call at the Houston airport, I felt emotions rise up in me like nothing I have ever experienced. The shock … the grief … the bewilderment. I could not process what had just happened. I sunk to the floor in tears, and my body started to go into a state of shock. My heart cried out the question, *How could this be?*

I had been sure I had heard God say that I should thank Him for her healing, and now she was dead. I believed God had given Lynn all the verses reminding her that the battle was not hers. She did not need to fear because the battle belongs to the Lord. I was devastated by the sober realization that I never got to say goodbye to my precious sister. The grief was almost more than I could bear.

Lynn had passed away around four thirty in the evening. Nearly two hours later, under the weight and shock of it all, we made our way from the Houston airport to the MD Anderson hospital as a very broken and shattered group of family members. It was dark out and raining hard. I stared out the shuttle van window through tears and disbelief. The rain made it seem like everything was weeping, even the sky.

I will never forget the overwhelming sense of grief I had in my heart as I entered that ICU room where her body lay still. I cannot even express the anguish we all felt as we stood around her bed, trying to wrap our minds around what had just happened. I lay in my hotel bed that night and pondered all these things. My head hurt so badly from crying, and sleep would not come to my aching heart.

The miracle we had been counting on did happen but not in the way we wanted it. Lynn was healed and is safely home with Jesus, but the rest of us who loved her so fiercely were left with shattered hearts. How could I handle this pain, this terrible disappointment, this unbelievable grief? I could get angry and lash out and shake my fist at God, or I could accept what He chose to do by calling her to heaven.

Like John the Baptist, I was questioning all that happened, and like the two on the road to Emmaus, I was discouraged, full of grief, and overwhelmed. I knew God had a much bigger picture in mind than I did, but the pain was unbearable. I had walked through the pain of a brain tumor and paralysis, through breast cancer and chemo, and through many other dark times, but this was by far the most painful thing I had ever experienced.

Lynn's days were over, and her work on earth was complete. Now she had been called to her eternal home by the Savior she so dearly loved. She had always said, "My days are already determined, and next to my birth date is my departure date, and nothing will hinder that. God has my days already numbered, and I am in His hand." She received a fabulous upgrade, but we who were left behind were broken. I felt like I still needed her here and was not ready to let her go so soon.

Once again, I was facing the decision of how to respond. In all honesty, I had a crisis of faith on the night of her death. My faith was being tested in the fire again. Here I was writing a chapter on being bitter or better, and right in the middle of it all, I found myself questioning God's decision to take my beloved sister from me. I was face-to-face with my unmet expectation of God. I had fully expected Him to heal her. We have expectations that God will not cross certain lines and that He will answer according to our requests, but the fact is He does not always answer the way we want. He has a much bigger plan in place, and He wants us to simply trust Him even when it hurts like crazy.

The days and weeks before Lynn passed I had spent hours in prayer and fasting seeking God's face for her healing. The message was to trust God no matter what. I was to trust in the loving kindness of God and believe God will give us what is best for us even if it isn't what we think we want. I thought about how Abraham must have questioned God's ways. He was promised a son, and God asked him to offer back this son as a sacrifice upon the altar. He trusted God, and Isaac, his son, was spared. Instead, God provided a ram that was caught in the thicket.

I reread the story in the Bible of the woman with the issue of blood and how she pushed through the crowds to get to Jesus to be healed. In my mind, I had been pushing through in prayer and fasting to bring my sister with her blood disease to His healing touch.

The revelation that I received from the Lord over the days following Lynn's passing was that my faith regarding her healing was in the wrong place. Like my prayers for Doris, I was praying for her complete healing here on earth. My faith, in Lynn's case, was in the answer that I wanted, not necessarily in the sovereignty of God who knew her time on earth was done. I had this head knowledge most of my life, but now I was being squeezed, and my heart was starting to speak. Did I really trust God's will on this? Did I trust in who God is or in what He could do for me? I realize now that my faith needs to be in God, believing He knows best because He can see the big picture.

There are false teachings in the world today that indicate you just need to have more faith and your loved one will be healed. I do not agree with this theology and believe that is where Christians get into dangerous waters. If miracles happen based on our performance, then we would get the credit not God. Lynn's passing was not because we did not have enough faith. Our faith in God should not be conditional or performance based but rather in the fact that He is God and He is sovereign.

How much better to include in our prayers, "This is what I desire God, but You know best." Jesus gave us a great example to follow in the Garden of Gethsemane when He asked His Father to remove the cup of suffering but ended his prayer, "Not My will, but Yours be done" (Luke 22:42 NKJV). In keeping with God's sovereign plan, the answer was for Jesus to go to the cross, and He suffered greatly to pay for our sins. If the answer to His prayer had been otherwise, our sins could not have been forgiven and our destiny would be eternity in hell.

It is God's bigger plan that we do not understand and often where we stumble. I think this is why we get discouraged and why we even falter at the bitter or better fork in the road. It is where I got discouraged and stalled for a while. After all, He is God, and He has the power to just speak a word and my sister Lynn could have been healed completely. I know He still performs miracles today, and some are healed while others are not. I know He loved Lynn and I know He loves me, so do I really trust God when it hurts so bad? Can I trust Him? The answer is *yes!*

If a person is born blind, that person does not know what sight is but he or she knows to depend on a guide who does see. The person willingly puts his or her hand into the hand of the seeing one and follows that person's leadership. This is like faith; we trust ourselves into the hands of Jesus because He can see where we are going. The problem is we don't realize we are blind to what lies ahead. When we truly believe in the sovereignty of God, we can follow Him, trusting that He is leading us down the right path.

After days of struggle and processing the shock of Lynn's passing, I was finally able to say, "God, You know best, and I thank You for that." When I made the decision to turn toward God and trust Him, then came peace and comfort. I miss my sister something fierce, and the pain in my heart is still very great, but I know she is in heaven and is more alive than she has ever been. I am very thankful that I will someday see her again because of what Jesus did on the cross. We both accepted His gift of salvation years ago, and our reunion is a definite thing, What an amazing comfort to know these painful separations are just temporary.

Death, disappointments, struggles, hurts, and fears are inevitable in this life. Our hope is in the one who came and is yet to come. God not only provides a remedy, but *He is the remedy*. What a comfort it is to know God is in total control of all things. He would not be omnipotent (all-powerful), omniscient (all-knowing), omnipresent (all-present), and omnibenevolent (all-loving and perfectly good) if He were not sovereign. He is so good and truly does all things right even when life gets so dark and you are blinded by the pain. He is the only true light in the dark.

> I will instruct you and teach you in the way you should go;
> I will counsel you with My loving eye on you.
>
> —Psalm 32:8 (NIV)

I Have Been Through The Valley Of Weeping

by L. B. Cowan

I have been through the valley of weeping,
The valley of sorrow and pain;
But the "God of all comfort" was with me,
At hand to uphold and sustain.

As we travel through life's shadowed valley,
Fresh springs of His love ever rise;
And we learn that our sorrows and losses,
Are blessings just sent in disguise.

SECTION 3
NAVIGATION

I have come that they might have life, and
that they might have it more abundantly.

—John 10:10 (NKJV)

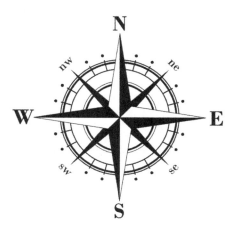

Dangerous Waters

Be sober, be vigilant; because your adversary the devil walks about
like a roaring lion, seeking whom he may devour.

—1 Peter 5:8 (NKJV)

One of my favorite jokes is about the guy who was learning to parachute.
He had taken all the training required, and it was time for his first
jump. After he jumped out of the plane, he pulled the parachute cord,
but nothing happened. Panicking, he pulled the emergency chute, but
again, nothing happened. As he was plummeting toward the earth,
he saw a speck moving up toward him. As he focused, he saw it was
another man, his clothes smoking and his hair singed. As they passed
midair, the skydiver shouted out, "Hey, do you know anything about
parachutes?" The singed guy replied, "No. Do you know anything
about propane stoves?"

This was especially funny to our family because of my dad's delayed
response when lighting the propane stove. I can remember our family
camping trips as a kid and watching my dad pump and pump the old
propane cookstove. After turning on the burner, he would take his
time to light a match. The pooling propane would light with a *kabam*.
His big bushy eyebrows would always take a beating. It was funny to
watch because nothing serious happened, but it could have led to a
terrible accident.

Sometimes in life, like the skydiver, we have plans that fail and we crash.
Other times, situations we're in can blow up in our faces. Although we

laugh at jokes like this, it is not so funny when it happens to us in real life. There have been many times in my life when my plans failed or blew up. Some of these experiences were caused by my own doing, while others were caused by someone else or by the enemy of our souls—Satan himself.

God has given us instruction in His word on how to navigate these trials. The problems come when we refuse to heed His advice. So often, we think we can just do it our own way, and when things blow up, we often get angry at God for our own failure to do it the right way. This is when we get into dangerous waters.

When navigating a boat, the captain can run aground if he does not heed the warning from his charts or navigation equipment. He can capsize quickly if he hits a reef or a shoal and tears a hole in the hull of the boat. So it is with our lives if we ignore God's instruction manual.

The Bible is full of instruction about keeping sin out of our lives. I have heard it said that *sin* adds to our troubles, subtracts from our energy, multiplies our difficulties, divides interest in our work, and has death as its wages (unless we have accepted God's salvation plan). Sin equals pain and not only hurts us but can also hurt the loved ones around us.

There are obvious sins that most everyone recognizes are wrong, like murder, stealing, lying, rape, and abuse. However, there are some sins, like gossip, anger, and slander, that might not seem as bad to us but can really choke up our communication and relationship with God. Through some of the dark times in my life, God has faithfully revealed to me some of the sins in my life that have really slowed up my progress as a Christian and caused me pain and suffering. There is nothing like trials in our lives to open our ears and eyes to some of the things that God desires for us to learn. These refining fires can help us to grow in our walks with Him.

Here are some of the hidden sins God showed me that put us in dangerous waters. They block the flow of His Spirit in our lives, and so often, we are not even aware that we are entertaining these dangerous habits.

I think one of the most subtle sins we allow into our lives that can really cause damage and choke up our progress as Christians is to harbor unforgiveness in our hearts. I have been so guilty of this sin, but God, in His faithfulness, has shown me how damaging it can be. I am constantly asking Him for help in this area. Unforgiveness starts with being offended by someone for something that person has done or said. If we do not immediately deal with that offense, it then turns to resentment, which leads to bitterness and an unforgiving spirit.

I've heard it said that offense is like picking up a rattlesnake and expecting to not get bit. There is an old Native American tale of a small child being persuaded by a rattlesnake to pick him up and help him out. After much persuasion and assurance that he would not bite, the child picked up the snake. Once the snake got what he wanted, he bit the child. Through tears and terror, the child cried out, "You bit me!" The snake replied, "You knew what I was when you picked me up."

So often, when we get hurt, we pick up the snake of offense. We pick it up knowing that it is a snake that bites, and yet we still pick it up. We were hurt, and we want to nurture that hurt. We feel so justified. There are so many ways we can be hurt by others. We are robbed, we are slandered, we are rejected, we are used, we are wounded, and we are harassed or abused by others, and the list goes on and on. This world is full of broken lives, and I have heard it said that hurting people hurt each other.

Unforgiveness has broken homes, families, marriages, businesses, friends, and churches. So many people are packing around hurts in their hearts and have not been able to let them go. Unforgiveness affects not only our relationships with each other but our prayer lives, our walks with God, and our health. I think a lot of illnesses can be tied to our thought lives and what is in our paradigms. According to Adrian Rogers, "Bitterness blows out the candles of joy and leaves the soul in darkness."

I have so enjoyed reading the stories of Corrie Ten Boom, a Christian woman who was a survivor of one of Hitler's worst concentration camps. She would often share her story and talk about the importance of forgiveness. In her book *Tramp for the Lord* she shares her favorite analogy of how God forgives our sins. She said it is like God casts our sins into the deepest ocean and they are gone forever, and then He places a sign out there that says: "No Fishing Allowed." Shortly after she finished sharing this analogy and her testimony to an audience in Germany, an older man in the group made his way toward her. She recognized him as one of the guards at the concentration camp where she had been so abused. He was one of the cruelest guards, and her mind flashed back to the memories of his abuse and the shame she felt having to walk naked past him.

He approached her and said, "How good it is to know that, as you say, all our sins are at the bottom of the sea!" He then thrust out his hand to shake hers.

What a test! She remembered the leather crop swinging from his belt. She was face-to-face with one of her captors, and her blood seemed to freeze. He went on to say, "I have become a Christian. I know that God has forgiven me for the cruel things I have done, but I would like to hear from your lips as well. Will you forgive me?"

Corrie remembered feeling nearly frozen with a coldness clutching her heart. Her beloved sister, Betsie, had died in that place. Could this man erase her slow, terrible death simply by asking? She wrestled in her soul but knew she had to forgive him. God's word commands us to forgive. She had seen firsthand the victims of Nazi brutality in Holland who were able to forgive their former enemies and then return to the outside world and rebuild their lives, no matter what the physical scars. Those who nursed their bitterness remained invalids. It was as simple and horrible as that.

Forgiveness is not an emotion. It is an act of the will, and the will can function regardless of the temperature of the heart. She cried out in silent prayer, *Jesus, help me!* She mechanically thrust her hand into his, and as she did, an incredible thing took place. There was a healing warmth that seemed to flood her whole being, bringing tears to her eyes. She said, "I forgive you, Brother, with all my heart." She said she had never known God's love so intensely as she did then. She tried to forgive in her own power but could not. It was the power of the Holy Spirit as recorded in Romans 5:5 (NKJV) "… because the love of God has been poured out in our hearts by the Holy Spirit who was given to us."

Lewis B. Smedes once said, "To forgive is to set the prisoner free and discover that the prisoner was you."

So often in life, we are hurt or offended and want to hang onto unforgiveness, especially if the offense is such a painful memory as was with Corrie. The Bible is so clear on the importance of letting things go and forgiving, even when forgiveness has not been asked for.

Ephesians 4:32 (NKJV) tells us: "And be kind to one another, tenderhearted, forgiving one another, even as God in Christ forgave you."

So how do we honestly forgive others when the pain in our hearts is as great as it was with Corrie? Humanly speaking, it is impossible to let go of enormous hurts, like forgiving the person who murdered a loved one or forgiving the abuser who violated you. How about forgiving the person who financially destroyed you or the spouse who cheated on you? I believe the only way to truly forgive is by the power of God inside of us. He works a miracle inside our hearts, but we first have to be willing to give these offenses to Him. Our sinful nature (the flesh) wants to hang onto the hurt. We want the offender to suffer and to pay back what he or she took. It is only by the power of the Holy Spirit that we can forgive others, and when we allow Him to work in and through us, miracles happen and we are healed and set free.

It is so very sad to see families and homes forever ruined and relationships broken because people will not forgive; they just will not let the offense go. Unforgiveness is like eating poison and expecting the other person to die. It is so important to let God heal us in all areas of our lives and in our relationships with others.

I've had broken relationships where there was an offense taken on both sides but the other person will not forgive. We are called to forgive even if the one who caused the offense has not asked for forgiveness or even cares to restore the friendship. Sometimes we can forgive but need to put up boundaries, especially if the person is not safe or healthy to be around. If people want to control us or fix us, we may have to distance ourselves from them, but we are always to forgive. I have found that unforgiveness can be deceptive. We think we have let it go, but then it raises its ugly head again and we have to deal with those hurt feelings again. God is the only one who can heal us and help us to completely let go and forgive.

Jesus gave us an amazing example to follow regarding forgiveness. He is one of the three in the Trinity. He is God the Son and came to earth as a baby, born in a borrowed manager. He was betrayed by his friends and unjustly accused by the religious leaders of that day. He was beaten, mocked, and spit upon and then crucified on a cross. He could have called ten thousand angels and wiped out all His enemies, but He obeyed His Father's will and took the punishment for all of our sins. He was dying for the very ones who were spitting on Him and putting the nails in His hands. He hung there on the hill that He had created for those that were breathing His air and using it to curse Him. He was God's perfect and spotless Lamb sacrificed for our redemption. 1 Peter 1:18–19 (NKJV) says, "Knowing that you were not redeemed with corruptible things, like silver or gold ... but with the precious blood of Christ, as of a lamb without blemish and without spot." While hanging on the cross Jesus said, "Father, forgive them; for they know not what they do." Luke 23:34 (KJV).

Jesus died in our place and was buried in a borrowed tomb. Three days later, He arose from out of the tomb and conquered death. Through His death and resurrection, He is offering us all forgiveness of our sins if we will accept Him. Jesus showed us the ultimate example of forgiveness.

Forgiveness is vital in the Christian's life. If we allow unforgiveness to reside, it will block the flow of the Holy Spirit in our lives. Unforgiveness keeps us as prisoners and can affect every part of our lives—especially our relationships. We must let God heal our broken hearts and emotions and let the hurt and the pain blow away in the winds of His grace and mercy.

The sin of strife is another area that puts us in dangerous waters. We live in a world of strife and anger. We witness people with road rage to those with ongoing family feuds. All around us there are couples getting divorced or children who are angry with their parents. There are church splits and religious wars and countries trying to blow each other up. The Bible is full of stories about strife and the damage it caused. God set out with a plan for His creation, and we have rebelled and messed it all up with our sinful ways. Strife is not God's plan. He calls us to be peacemakers and maintainers of peace. How is this possible when we live in a world where people are so angry? It is only possible when God's Holy Spirit is inside of us. We are sinners with an old sin nature that loves to bicker about things. We all want to be right and defend ourselves. We often find it hard to turn the other cheek or let God be our defender.

We are told to stand up for what is right and to defend the truth of God, but it must be done with humility and a right heart. It is the angry or proud attitude of the heart that will cause strife. We will have disagreements and not everyone will see it our way, but it is how we handle those disagreements that can be a problem and that is where strife comes from.

Strife can break apart relationships and is one of Satan's biggest weapons against the Christian. He likes to divide and conquer. The Bible says a house divided cannot stand. It is so important to keep the strife out of our lives not only because God says to but for our own good and blessing.

The Bible talks about handling disagreements, and we are instructed to love each other with humility. We are to think of others more highly than ourselves (Philippians 2:3 NKJV). "A soft answer turns away wrath" (Proverbs 15:1 NKJV). Without God, this is nearly impossible. We need to be empowered by His Holy Spirit in order to keep the strife away. We all struggle with our own pride and want to have the last word. We want to defend ourselves. When someone hurts us, we often want to hurt that person back. If we do not handle these attitudes with God's help, they usually end up in strife.

I heard a story once about a couple who lived in an apartment building with an outside balcony. The pigeons and doves would often land on the railing. Over time, they noticed that the pigeons would stay on the railing no matter what was going on inside, but the doves would fly away when there was any loud or angry voices coming from inside. The illustration was used to describe how the dove was like the Holy Spirit is in our lives. As Christians, we are indwelt by His Spirit when we become part of His family. The Holy Spirit of God is referred to in the Bible as a dove. We disrupt our communion with His Spirit when we have strife or any other hidden sin in our lives. He is still there, but we will not hear that still small voice as clearly as we would if we had judged the sin in our lives.

My dad used to say, "Keep short accounts with God." We are all going to mess up in life, but we should address the mistakes quickly and get back in communion with God. We need to be sure we do not let bad behaviors continue and should not go to bed angry.

> If we confess our sins, He is faithful and just to forgive us our sins and to cleanse us from all unrighteousness. (1 John 1:9 NKJV)

> Be angry, and do not sin. Do not let the sun go down on your wrath. (Ephesians 4:26 NLT)

I heard a funny story about a guy who was stranded on an island for many years. One day he spotted a ship and immediately built a fire on the beach and generated as much smoke as possible. It worked! Soon, the ship was headed his way. The man on the island was overjoyed and met his rescuers as they landed. After some preliminary conversation, the man in charge asked the man on the island how he had survived for so many years alone. The man replied by telling of his exploits finding food and how he was able to make a fine house to live in.

In fact, the man said, "You can see my home from here. It's up there on the ridge." He pointed the men in the direction of his home. They looked up and saw three buildings. They inquired about the building next to the man's house, and he replied, "That's my church. I go there to worship on Sundays." When asked about the third building, the man replied, "That's where I used to go to church."

Even though this story is fictional and funny, the message is profound. Everywhere I go, there I am. We are all prone to have strife, even if it is with ourselves. We need God's help and His power on the inside of us to keep the strife out of our lives. Always being right is overrated. We need to do it God's way and take the high road. If we keep the friction out of our lives and allow the anointing of the Holy Spirit, we won't overheat. Sometimes keeping the peace is harder than winning the war.

Psalm 119:165 (KJV) tells us, "Great peace have they which love thy law and nothing shall offend them."

The Bible offers no promise of peace to people living outside of God's will. To be at peace with God, we must deal with any disobedience in our lives. There are so many habits or things we do that we might not even be aware of that are sinful. Do we have critical or judgmental attitudes? Are we gossiping or slandering another person? So many people lie to each other without even batting an eye, and yet it's one of the sins that God says He hates. Another area that we sin in is talking negatively about ourselves or others. Our words are so important, and we can speak life or death. The book of Proverbs is full of instruction about our words and how important they are. They can build up, or they can tear down. Like a hammer, our words have power to build something or destroy it. God cares greatly how we treat each other and what we say about each other.

So often, we get comfortable with our own sins but are so critical of others. Matthew 7:1 (NKJV) says, "Judge not that ye be not judged." Sin is sin, and we are all sinners. The Bible calls us to love each other, pray for one another, and encourage each other in the Lord.

One of the things God hates is pride, especially religious pride. We need to remember that as followers of Jesus Christ, we are all sinners saved by grace. Not one of us is saved by good works. We are all a bunch of cracked pots. Humility is to make a right estimate of one's self. Blessings come from obedience, but we need to never think we have earned them.

We should never look down on others and have a haughty attitude. If someone has fallen into sin or has lost his or her way, we should rather pray for that person and love the individual back to health. (James 5:19–20). The minute we think we are better than another, we are on a slippery slope. We are all capable of falling into sin, and everybody has a breaking point. It is only by God's grace that we do anything right. It is Him and Him alone who can keep us from falling apart. We, by our very nature, are sinners, and that is what we do—we sin. It is only by His Holy Spirit on the inside of us that gives us the strength to overcome sin.

There is an example in the Bible of two men praying. One man was a Pharisee and the other a tax collector. The Pharisee was raving about all his good deeds and thanking God that he wasn't as bad as everyone else. The tax collector hung his head and exclaimed, "God, be merciful to me a sinner." It goes on to say that the tax collector went home justified, rather than the other.

> For everyone who exalts himself will be humbled, but the one who humbles himself will be exalted. (Luke 18:14 NKJV)

Another hidden sin is one of being discontent. Sometimes we struggle with this sin and don't even realize it. Before my brain tumor surgery, I was working hard on expanding our ranch. I was driven to buy more land and more cattle. I had lost my vision on what was really important to God. I was not content and wanted more and more. We criticize others for this sin when we see it in them, but we quite often have it in our own lives and are not even aware of it. It is good to do a regular inventory and ask ourselves the question, "Why am I doing this?" Is this for my kingdom or for God's kingdom? There is nothing wrong with expansion, but it does become a problem when it is all about being greedy or having a discontented spirit. As a follower of Jesus, my focus here on planet Earth should be to tell those who are on the road to hell about the amazing gift of salvation that God has offered to us.

Living the abundant life Jesus offers us is being thankful and content for what He has already blessed us with. Contentment is a learned behavior. The apostle Paul wrote while in prison, "for I have learned in whatever state I am, to be content" (Philippians 4:11 NKJV). A thankful heart is a happy heart. It is so easy to focus on what we don't have rather than on what we do have. Sometimes it is not until we lose something that we took for granted that we realize just how much we have to be thankful for.

I remember staring at my left leg after my brain surgery, trying to get it to move, but there was no response. I had never really thought about my legs being able to move and being thankful for that. My nephew Michael, with his advanced stage multiple sclerosis, sits in a motorized wheelchair every day and depends on others to feed him. He blows through a straw to operate his iPad, and yet he has a thankful heart. How is this humanly possible? It is because he trusts God and knows that He is bigger than his handicap. He has God's Holy Spirit living inside of him that gives him supernatural strength. Michael is content and looking forward to heaven. He has an amazing future ahead of him because he has accepted God's plan of salvation.

How often do we thank God for what we do have? If we are followers of Christ, we have so much to be thankful for. Most of all, we can be so thankful we are not going to hell but will spend our eternity with Jesus!

> I once cried out for a new pair of shoes until I saw a man who had no feet. (Randy L. McClave)

Life is not about obtaining more stuff. Life is all about Jesus and what He has done for us. Life here on earth is about preparing us for the eternal life to come. We need to ask God for help to be thankful every day, no matter what our circumstances are. We need to ask for His help to stay out of the dangerous waters of sin and keep clear communication with Him.

> But godliness with contentment is great gain.
> —1 Timothy 6:6 (NIV)

We Two

by Emily P. Miller

"I cannot do it alone;
The waves run fast and high,
And the fogs close all around,
The light goes out in the sky;
But I know that we two
Shall win in the end,
Jesus and I.

"Coward and wayward and weak,
I change with the changing sky;
Today so eager and bright,
Tomorrow too weak to try;
But He never gives in,
So we two shall win,
Jesus and I.

"I could not guide it myself,
My boat on life's wild sea;
There's One who sits by my side,
Who pulls and steers with me.
And I know that we two
Shall safe enter port,
Jesus and I."

THE POWER TOOL OF PRAYER

This is the confidence we have in approaching God: that if we ask
anything according to His will, He hears us.

—1 John 5:14 (NIV)

My dad loved to tell the hilarious story of a guy who bought a chain
saw from his local hardware store. He took it home, and that first day
he really struggled to cut up his firewood. It took him all day to just
get through one log. So the next day he took the chain saw back to the
hardware store and complained that there must be something wrong.
The salesman took the saw and gave the start cord a mighty tug. The
chain saw fired up with a loud roar, and the guy jumped back and
yelled, "Hey, what's that noise?!" My dad would laugh every time he
told this story, which, in turn, would make us laugh along with him.

Although this fictional story is funny and makes for a good laugh, it
would be impossible to manually cut wood with a chain saw without
the power source of the engine. A power tool without its power source
is useless. So it is with the follower of Christ; we are not designed to do
life without His help and His power inside of us.

God has given His followers a toolbox of power tools. One of the most
powerful tools we have is the Holy Spirit who indwells us, giving us
His power to rise above our circumstances. He has also given us His
Word, the Bible, which gives us instruction on how to navigate life. It
is referred to as the sword of the Spirit, alongside the other pieces of the
Christians armor in Ephesians 6.

> For the word of God is living and powerful, and
> sharper than any two-edged sword, piercing even
> to the division of soul and spirit, and of joints and
> marrow, and is a discerner of the thoughts and intents
> of the heart. (Hebrews 4:12 NKJV)

We are also given the fruit of the Spirit, which are love, joy, peace, patience, kindness, goodness, faithfulness, gentleness, and self-control (Galatians 5:22–23). These fruits of the Spirit are oftentimes developed within us through the trials in our life.

Another power tool we have is prayer. Prayer is our ability to talk with God. What an amazing privilege it is to take our needs or requests and ask our omnipotent God for help. Prayer is engaging the power source. We so often try to cut through the trials of life, like the man with the powerless saw, without even thinking to pray. How much easier it is to have the power source engaged.

My prayer life changed during the winter of 1993. We were living in central Washington and attending a small church in the town of Ellensburg. Our pastor gave everyone in the congregation a small prayer journal at the end of the year and encouraged each one of us to take prayer seriously by using this journal. Beginning in January 1994, I began the habit of using a prayer journal. It was a simple discipline, but the power of seeing God work has greatly changed my view of prayer. The answers have not always been what I have wanted to hear, but God is faithful, and I am finding that His way is always best even if I initially did not think so.

My prayer journal method was simple; I would write the date and prayer request down and then talk to God about it in prayer. When the answer came, I would write that below the request and then cross it off. I quickly filled that first small journal and bought another. I finally converted to a small three-ring notebook that can easily be updated with new pages. I would have to say that looking back over the last twenty-five years, this has been one of the most life-changing things I have ever done. It has radically changed me, and I can say with confidence that prayer changes things.

Over the years, God showed me that I did not need to keep repeating myself to Him every day with the same request but rather pray about it and then thank Him for the answer that was on the way. My daily prayers have turned into help for the day—for guidance and direction not only for myself but for those that I pray for. I am learning to pray with thanksgiving that He has heard me and is working on the answer.

When life falls apart or we need direction or help, why is it that prayer seems to be the last thing we do? Why don't we pick up this power tool and get help? It has taken me many years to finally figure out that prayer should be the first thing we do, and it is by far the most powerful thing we can do. No one accomplishes so much in so little time as when he or she is praying. Prayer is one of our greatest privileges and is vital in our walk with God!

God clearly states in His word, "Pray without ceasing" (1 Thessalonians 5:17 NKJV) and to, "pray for one another" (James 5:16 NKJV).

Prayer is often looked at as a life preserver. We only think about praying when life falls apart and we need help. The craziest statement that we can ever use is, "Well, all we can do now is pray." Prayer should be the first and foremost thing we do. It is unleashing the power of heaven and seeking direction from the one who knows what is up ahead.

Prayer is one of the most powerful things we can do and one of the most under-utilized resources. I have heard it said that prayer is like a handclasp with God. It is communicating with your Creator—the one who holds your heartbeat in His hand. Why would anyone not want to talk with the one who has all power? Prayer is a powerful tool of communication with God, and it opens the door for Him to work.

I have learned and am continuing to learn to use this powerful tool of prayer in my life. It is how I like to start my day, and I find it to be a comforting thing to talk to God all throughout the day. If we are going to be in a relationship with someone, wouldn't it be vital to communicate? It would be super strange to be in a relationship with someone and not talk. The relationship would not last long, and it wouldn't even be a relationship. How can we get to know someone if we do not talk to each other? The same is true with knowing God. He wants us to be in relationship with Him. Prayer is the amazing tool we have to communicate with Him.

Prayer is not a bunch of fancy words; it is a heartfelt, honest conversation with God. Some prayers are just a simple, "God, help me!" He already knows our thoughts and our hearts, so we just need to be honest with Him. If we are hurting or we are offended at Him, He wants to help us through. Talk to Him; He's just a prayer away! When we are confused, we need to ask Him for direction and revelation. There is nothing too big or too small to pray about. He wants to be close to us, and He desires to be a part of our lives.

I have learned to use this power tool of prayer when I hit those scary crossroads in my life. They are big decisions that can completely change the outcome of life. I have spent many hours seeking God's face through prayer and fasting and have always found Him to be faithful and true. God answers prayer!

So often in life, we think we know what to do or we know the answers when a problem or decision comes up, but we don't take the time to pray about it and ask for God's guidance. I have found out the hard way that it is best to seek God for direction even if the answer seems like a *no-brainer*. One of the best things to say is, "God, please go before me. Please show me what to do and clear the way or close the door." Many times I have prayed this way and found out that He took me a different way than I would have chosen. Other times the door may get closed. Sometimes it has been clear sailing. He is faithful to show up when we pray. Prayer is depending on God to navigate. It is like letting Him be at the helm. When we don't pray, we show an independent spirit, saying, "God, I don't need Your help here."

As I have studied prayer and as I have prayed through some stormy seas in my own life, I have come to realize that prayer is not only an incredibly powerful tool but is vital to my relationship with the Lord. I have also learned that prayer is not to be considered a vending machine where you feed in our requests and out pops the desired result. Prayer is not room service in a hotel. It is asking God for help and for direction but also being surrendered to His decision on what is best for my life.

Letting God be God is where we often stumble. This is where, so many times, we get offended at God or we give up on prayer because the thing we were asking for did not happen like we expected. I had this happen when I was praying for my sister's healing. I asked God to heal her body from disease, but she died.

I prayed fervently that I would not have to have chemo when diagnosed with breast cancer, but my answer from the Lord was, "Trust me through treatment." This was not the answer I wanted, but it was God's answer. Many times when our prayers are not answered the way we want them to be answered, we say, "Well, that didn't work," or, "That was just a waste of time," or, worse yet, "God must not love me." It is never a waste of time to talk to God, and He does care and loves us deeply.

Corrie Ten Boom, in her book *Tramp for the Lord*, talks about earnestly praying that God would not allow her to be sent to a German concentration camp. Not only did she get sent to Germany, but Corrie was sent to one of the worst camps called Ravensbrück. It was a concentration camp that was known for its filthy, inhumane conditions and treatment. God had much bigger plans for Corrie. He had a mission field for her, and she led numerous women to Jesus during her stay there. There were so many precious women who had no hope during those days and who are now in heaven because of Corrie's faithfulness in sharing the news of God's plan of salvation.

Corrie could have given up on prayer, but she didn't. She continued to pray and ask for God's help. Her life was an amazing testimony to God's care in the midst of horrible circumstances. He faithfully answered her prayers and eventually delivered her when His work for her in that place was done. Great will be her reward for faithful service to God.

Another incredible example of prayer was when George Müller, a Christian evangelist in the 1800s, was on a steamer ship bound for Quebec. They were off the banks of Newfoundland, and the fog was dense and traveling was slow. It was Wednesday, and George Müller approached the captain and said, "I need to be in Quebec for a speaking engagement on Saturday."

The captain told George that would be impossible at the rate they were going.

"Very well," Müller said. "If your ship can't take me, God will find some other means of locomotion to take me. I have never broken an engagement in fifty-seven years." He continued, "Let us go down to the chart room and pray."

The captain, who was also a Christian, looked at him like he was a lunatic. He said, "Mr. Müller, do you know how dense the fog is?"

"No," he replied. "My eye is not on the density of the fog but on the living God who controls every circumstance of my life." George Müller then got down on his knees and prayed a very simple prayer asking God to remove the fog immediately. When he was finished praying, the captain was going to pray, but George Müller stopped him and told him not to pray.

"First, you do not believe He will, and second, I believe He has. Captain," he continued, "I have known my Lord for fifty-seven years, and there has never been a single day that I have failed to gain an audience with the King. Get up, Captain, and open the door, and you will find the fog is gone."

The captain got up and found that, in fact, the fog was completely gone. On Saturday afternoon, George Müller arrived in Quebec. Like George, we need to pray believing in an all-powerful God.

Here are a few things I've learned about this power tool called prayer:

1. Sin in our lives can damage our communication with God. If we want our prayers to be more powerful, then we need to keep the pipes clean—that is, keep the sin out of our lives. Hidden sins like unforgiveness can really affect our prayer lives and delay answers. I know this firsthand, as I have struggled with unforgiveness, and it has blocked the flow of the Holy Spirit in my life. Living in sin or allowing hidden sins in our lives can be major blockers to hearing from God.
   The prayer of the upright is His delight. (Proverbs 15:8 NKJV)

   The effective, fervent prayer of a righteous man avails much. (James 5:16 NKJV)

   If I regard iniquity in my heart, The Lord will not hear. (Psalm 66:18 NKJV)

2. We should ask two things of ourselves before praying about something.
   a. Is this request consistent with God's word? Obviously we would not pray for things we know to go against the Word of God.

b.   Is this God's will for my life? Some things we know are not God's will according to what is taught in His Word.

Nothing lies beyond the reach of prayer except those things outside the will of God. (Phillip Brooks)

This is the confidence we have in approaching God: that if we ask anything according to His will, He hears us. (1 John 5:14 NIV)

3.   Pray believing. Have faith that a sovereign God will answer our prayers according to His will. Trust in who God is not in what He can do for us. Let us come boldly with faith believing *in* God!

Faith sees the invisible, believes the unbelievable and receives the impossible. (Corrie Ten Boom)

And whatever things you ask in prayer, believing, you will receive. (Matthew 21:22 NKJV)

4.   Give up the right to know why or understand His direction regarding the answer to our prayers. We need to accept the truth that God is in control, and His ways are higher than our ways.

"For My thoughts are not your thoughts, Nor are your ways My ways," says the Lord. "For as the heavens are higher than the earth, So are My ways higher than your ways, and My thoughts than your thoughts." (Isaiah 55:8–9 NKJV)

5.   Pray with humility. Do not come to God proud, presumptuous, or arrogant. Do not focus on what He can do for us but rather focus on who He is.

Holy, holy, holy, is the Lord God Almighty, who was and is and is to come! (Revelation 4:8 ESV)

And He is before all things, and in Him all things hold together. (Colossians 1:17 ESV)

When pride comes, then comes shame; but with the humble is wisdom. (Proverbs 11:2 NKJV)

6. Pray with thanksgiving. We need to get a revelation of whom we are talking to. What a phenomenal privilege to be able to communicate with Almighty God, our Creator and the one who holds our very breath in His hands. Be thankful that He knows best. Be thankful that we do not always get our own way. Be thankful that He knows the end from the beginning and can see ahead. Be thankful for the answers that are already on the way. Can you even imagine what it would be like if we couldn't pray?

   Continue earnestly in prayer, being vigilant in it with thanksgiving. (Colossians 4:2 NKJV)

7. Pray continually. Pray about everything! Never underestimate the power of prayer. It is vital for survival in this world!

   Pray without ceasing. (1 Thessalonians 5:17 NKJV)

8. Pray in the name of Jesus. It is acknowledging our position in Him. We pray in His authority, which is kind of like having power of attorney. We are representatives of Him. There is tremendous power in His name. The Bible is full of examples of the power in His name; demons were cast out, people were healed, and miracles happened in His name. Praying in Jesus's name means praying according to God's will. It's praying for things that will honor and glorify Jesus.

> And whatever you ask in My name, that I will do,
> that the Father may be glorified in the Son. If you ask
> anything in My name, I will do it. (John 14:13–14
> NKJV)

I thank my parents for teaching me the value of prayer and my pastor for encouraging me to keep a prayer journal. Prayer is not only a power tool; it is a weapon! I use it every day in my life, and since I have developed this habit, it has revolutionized my journey. I encourage everyone to engage this power tool in their life. It is a life-changing habit!

> The Lord is near to all who call on Him,
> to all who call on Him in truth.
>
> —Psalm 145:18 (NKJV)

The Power of Prayer

by John Newton

Wrestling prayer can wonders do,
Bring relief in deepest straits;
Prayer can force a passage through
Iron bars and brazen gates.
by John Newton

Prayer changes things—those bound by fear,
need doubt no more when God is near.
Prayer changes things—does it seem odd,
that prayer should move the hand of God?

"SMART LIVING"

The thief (Satan) does not come except to
steal, and to kill, and to destroy.
I (Jesus) have come that they may have life, and
that they may have it more abundantly.

—John 10:10 (NKJV)

The traffic was bad that Friday night with so many people heading out of town for the weekend. My sister had just left work and was heading home. As she approached the on-ramp to the freeway, she noticed that she was low on fuel, so she turned around and again was delayed by this heavy traffic. As she pulled into the gas station, she noticed a young boy walking down the sidewalk going right by the mini-market station. As she got out of the car to fuel up, she had a very strong thought. *Buy that kid a Coke.* She thought to herself, *Where did that thought come from? This seems crazy! Why would I do that? I don't even know this kid, and he would probably think I'm nuts.*

The thought persisted, and she had an overwhelming sense that she needed to obey. She continued to argue with herself but finally yelled out at the boy who had now made his way down the street, "Hey, you! Come here." As he approached her car she said, "I would like to buy you a Coke."

His face exploded into a smile. "That's my sweet Jesus! Lady, I was just walking by here, and I was praying that I might be able to have a Coke."

My sister was speechless. She was in the middle of a divine encounter between God and a thirteen-year-old boy. She was being used as God's hands and feet. This message she received was the Holy Spirit inside of her prompting her to bless this kid. She had no idea that he had just prayed for a Coke, and it was specifically a Coke, not a Sprite or a Root beer but a Coke.

The two of them entered that mini-mart with joy in their hearts. This little guy was praising Jesus the whole way for the amazing answer to his prayer, and my sister was overwhelmed with joy that God had prompted her like that. She bought him the biggest size Coke in the store and candy too. She offered him a ride home and heard his incredibly sad story. His father was in prison, and his mother was ill and unable to work. He had a paper route because money was tight, and so a Coke was definitely a luxury. What a thrill and a blessing for my sister to be in the middle of this divine appointment.

When we accept God's plan of salvation and are spiritually born, He gives the Holy Spirit to us. What we do with that power is up to us. We can suppress it by living in sin or by not inviting Him to help us, or we can engage this power by allowing Him to work through us. In order for Him to work through us, we need to get out of the way and give Him access to every area of our lives. This means allowing Him to be the Lord of our lives. Being indwelt by the Holy Spirit is different than being empowered by Him. God has given us this amazing power, and yet we often live wimpy, pathetic lives, struggling to get by. He wants us to enjoy life abundantly.

There is a story of a poor elderly couple who had saved up their money to take an all-inclusive trip on a cruise ship. The day finally came when they were able to buy their tickets. They boarded the luxury vessel and settled in for their cruise. At the end of the seven days they were seen carrying a moldy bag of food. When someone questioned why they had this disgusting sack, they replied, "Well, there's no way we could afford the food on this trip too!" Thinking they had to bring their own food with them, they had missed the abundance of all the gourmet buffets on the ship for the entire journey. We read this story and think how crazy that is, but really it is no different than Christians who are trying to do life without the blessings that are available through the power of the Holy Spirit. God has so much for us to enjoy, and He wants us to partner with Him.

This abundant life Jesus offers His children could be termed *smart living*. Everything today seems to be labeled *smart something*. There are *smartphones*, *smart packaging*, *smart televisions*, and even *smart cars*. These *smart products* have the ability to think or perform with the use of computerization or some sort of *smart* technology.

With God's Holy Spirit inside of us, we can do things that we couldn't do on our own. We can rise above the storm like my friend Doris did. We can forgive like Corrie Ten Boom was able to forgive the guard. With God living on the inside of us, we have tremendous power available to us that can give us peace and comfort during those gut-wrenching circumstances that often come our way. It is the power that can heal us and set us free completely. We have His power to be victorious in every situation if we will ask Him for His help.

The lordship of Christ is letting go and letting God. Surrender is hard for us as humans. We, by nature, are afraid to let go. We want our own way, and we want life to turn out the way we think would be best. I read an old story about a little girl who bought a pearl necklace at the dime store. She had saved up almost two dollars to buy these pearls, and after purchasing them, she wore them constantly. She loved those pearls. Every night before bed, her dad would read her a story. One night when he finished the story, he asked his little girl, "Do you love me?"

She quickly responded, "Oh yes, Daddy, you know that I love you."

He said, "Then can I have your pearls?"

She cried, "Oh, Daddy, not my pearls."

This went on for several nights. Then one night, when her dad came to read her the bedtime story, he noticed she was very sad and had tears rolling down her cheeks. He tenderly asked, "What's the matter?"

She held up her pearl necklace to give him. "Here, Daddy. You can have my necklace."

He took the necklace with one hand, and with his other hand, he reached into his pocket and pulled out a blue velvet case with a strand of genuine pearls and gave them to her. He was just waiting for her to give up the dime-store stuff so he could give her the genuine treasure. Sometimes we are like this little girl, wanting to tightly hang onto our worldly treasure that we think will make us happy. When we do this, we miss out on the genuine treasure God desires to give us.

The first thing He wants us to let go of is our own way. He wants us to accept His free gift of salvation and receive life eternal in heaven. We do this by confessing to Him that we have sinned and we believe and accept His Son, Jesus, as the only one who can save us from our sins. Once we do that, we become part of His family. We now belong to Him, and we become followers of Jesus. Our sins are forgiven (past, present, and future), and our destiny is fixed! We have a home in heaven and eternal life with Him. This is an amazing exchange. We give up our sins and receive complete forgiveness. We forfeit hell and get life eternal in heaven. It is the deal of a lifetime!!

> For whoever desires to save his life will lose it, but whoever loses his life for My sake will find it. For what profit is it to a man if he gains the whole world, and loses his own soul? Or what will a man give in exchange for his soul? (Matthew 16:25–26 NKJV)

The next thing God asks us to give up is ourselves. He desires that we mature as Christians and become conformed to Him—to become like Jesus. In order to do that, we have a lot of refining to go through. He wants to take up residence on the inside of us, but that means the flesh (or the old sin nature) has to move out. He wants us to die to ourselves and allow Him to give us that abundant life that He died to give us. He wants us to allow the Holy Spirit to rule and reign in our lives. This means allowing His Lordship in every area of our lives. He gives us beauty for ashes (Isa. 61:3). He can take our mess and make a miracle. We give up our weaknesses for His unbelievable power. We give up our sorrow for joy unspeakable. We give up our poverty for riches untold.

There is a story about a monkey who would put his hand in the candy jar, and when he clutched the candy, his fist was too big to pull back out through the mouth of the jar. If he would just let go of the candy, he could be free and escape the oncoming captors. We are like the monkey, thinking that if let go we are going to lose out. However, with God, when we let go and give Him our messes, He gives us the miracle of new life in Him. We receive healing in every area of our lives. He can make all things new.

We can have *smart living* by allowing God's Holy Spirit to empower us and guide us through life, or we can try to struggle through in our own strength. Doing life God's way is the only way. Allowing Him to live in us and through us is the only way to live victoriously. He has the power to lift us up above the storm and give us victory in all things. He is the light behind the dark shadows that come into our lives.

> This world for the believer is not a big playfield for
> pleasure but rather a battlefield to discover and use His
> power. It is not a resort town for rest and relaxation
> but a battlefield to gain the victory in Christ.
> —Bill O'Brien

> And if the Spirit of Him who raised Jesus from the dead is living
> in you, He who raised Christ from the dead will also give life
> to your mortal bodies because of His Spirit who lives in you.
> —Romans 8:11 (NIV)

Colleen Anthony

The Touch of the Master's Hand

by Myra Brooks Welch

T'was battered and scarred, and the auctioneer
thought it hardly worth his while
To waste his time on the old violin,
but he held it up with a smile.
"What am I bidden, good folks", he cried,
"Who'll start the bidding for me?"
A dollar, a dollar, then two! Only two?
Two dollars, and who'll make it three?
Three dollars, once; three dollars, twice;
Going for three …"
But, no,
From the room far back, a grey-haired man
Came forward and picked up the bow;
Then, wiping the dust from the old violin,
And tightening up the strings,
He played a melody pure and sweet
As a caroling angel sings.

The music ceased, and the auctioneer,
With a voice that was quiet and low, said:
"What now am I bid for this old violin?"
As he held it up with the bow.
"A thousand dollars, and who'll make it two?"
"Two thousand! And who'll make it three?"
"Three thousand, once, three thousand, twice;
And going and gone," said he.

The people cheered, but some of them cried,
"We do not quite understand, what changed its worth?"
Swift came the reply;
"The Touch of the Master's Hand."

And many a man with life out of tune
And battered and scarred with sin,
Is auctioned cheap to the thoughtless crowd
Much like the old violin
A mess of pottage, a glass of wine;
A game—and he travels on.
He's going once, and going 'twice,
He's 'going and almost gone.'
But the Master comes and the foolish crowd
Never can quite understand
The worth of a soul and the change that's wrought
By The Touch of the Master's Hand.

LOG BOOK

Those who listen to instruction will prosper;
those who trust the Lord will be joyful.

—Proverbs 16:20 (NLT)

Years ago, I was on a business trip flying from Boston to Maine. The flight had been delayed due to weather, and there was a chance that it was going to be canceled. Finally, it was announced that we were just ahead of the storm and clearance had been given. We boarded the plane, and off we went. It was a small commuter plane with two seats on one side and a single seat on the other. Not long after we were in the air, the storm overtook us, causing the small plane to take quite a beating. It was one scary ride, and I wondered if we were going to make it.

I often flew with my job but had never experienced this kind of storm while in the air. We could see the lightning flashing all around us, and the turbulence was intense. The plane would shutter and then slam down like it was free-falling. I am sure it was only slightly dropping, but it felt like we were dropping out of the sky. The noise of the plane creaking in the storm was definitely unnerving. Most of the passengers on board wore troubled looks, and it seemed like we were all clutching our seats. I looked down at the dark waters of the Atlantic Ocean and wondered if this was the day I would meet my maker. The sky was dark and so was the water. The conditions outside were frigid, and I wondered if we went down and survived the impact in the waters below how long we could stay alive in such cold temperatures. In the seats ahead of me were two young men who were completely terrified. One of them was making all kinds of noises when the plane would drop. His guttural noises added another level of fear to the already frayed nerves of the other passengers. The guy was a complete basket case and was squeezing the juice, so to speak, out of the seat in front of him. It was a terrifying flight! Thankfully, we landed safely, and there was a loud applause when the wheels bounced down on the runway in Portland, Maine.

I have never forgotten the terror we all felt when we thought we might not make it. It is normal and natural to feel fear when things like this happen. This particular situation turned out safely, but sometimes there are events in life that do not end as well and we are forced to face tragedy or terrible disappointment. Like the man on the airplane, our response to a trial can be full-blown terror. Other times, it may be anger or unbelievable grief or even disbelief. Sometimes we are just completely overwhelmed and discouraged. All of these emotions are normal, but it is how we act after the initial shock and what we truly believe that decides which fork in the road we are going to travel down.

In the first chapter of this book, I mentioned that God was about to reset my life sail and change my paradigm about Him. As I look back over the last twenty-five years, the changes He has helped me make have been significant. Some of the life storms I have been through have been terrifying like the Boston flight, and many times I have wondered if I would survive. With each of these storms, I have experienced God's presence and His protection. He has been with me in the dark whether I was aware of it or not. As I have grown in my faith, I have sensed His presence more and more and have learned that He is always present.

Had this Boston flight gone down, the authorities would have tried to recover the plane's log book, which is known as the *little black box*. It would have told the authorities what happened onboard just before the crash. Log books are used in many different applications and are a way to record important events, operation, navigation, changes in protocol, and other information. I started to keep a log book of my life back in

1994. I started with a daily planner and then around the year 2007 added a journal notebook. It is amazing to look back at some of those early entries and see the changes that have happened in my paradigm. I believe keeping a journal is a good way to bring focus to what it is we truly believe. It has helped me to sort through some of the false paradigms in life and clearly see how God has redirected my life sail.

When my life sail started to shift in 1996, I took a step of faith and invited Jesus to be Lord of my life. He was my Savior, but at the time I was not allowing His complete lordship. I heard a message on the five *D*s of lordship that helped me to understand this concept better. The first *D* was to *decide* that we want Jesus to be Lord. This is where a lot of people hesitate. We don't want to lose control of our own destiny or plans and dreams. The second *D* was to *denounce* any unjudged sin in our lives. The third *D* was to *die* to ourselves. That means to let go of what is important to us and embrace what is important to God. The fourth *D* was to be *disciplined* to feed on the word of God. In order for us to know who God is, we need to read His word. The fifth *D* *was* to *declare* His lordship. Lordship is letting go and letting God. It is surrendering our life into God's hands. It is like saying, "Lord, I will do or say, go or stay, or give whatever You want me to—no reservations, no conditions." It's like the trucking company slogan that reads, "Any time, any place, any load."

> Then Jesus said to His disciples, "If anyone desires to come after Me, let him deny himself, and take up his cross, and follow Me." (Matthew 16:24 NKJV)

Around this time, God started a mighty revival in my life. In the fall of 1991, we were living in central Washington, and I was pregnant for the third time. We had lost our first two children to miscarriages, and I had been devastated by both. So this third pregnancy was being closely monitored. I had made it to the third trimester and seemed to be on track. However, during the last few months, I started to show signs of preeclampsia and was ordered to be on bed rest.

About a month before my due date I woke up with flulike symptoms. A quick trip to my doctor revealed that it was probably just the flu, but I was to call if symptoms got worse. Well, symptoms did get worse, and I found myself in the emergency room later that evening. After more testing, it was determined that I was suffering from appendicitis. An emergency surgery was scheduled to remove my appendix. We were so anxious because this precious premature child of ours would be exposed to x-rays and anesthesia while my appendix was removed. The surgery went well, but twenty-four hours later, things took a turn for the worse. My blood panel showed that my platelets were dangerously low; it was revealed that I had HELLP syndrome, and it hadn't been my appendix after all. This pregnancy complication is a severe condition that causes hemolysis (breakdown of red blood cells), elevates liver enzymes, and lowers platelet count. HELLP syndrome is fairly rare, so this country hospital I was at had never seen a case like mine before.

I was ushered back into surgery for an emergency cesarean section. I was told that if my platelets got much lower, they would not be able to operate on me. It was now very urgent to deliver the baby, or we could both die. I was also informed that I would need to be awake while they intubated me. I innocently asked what intubation was, as I had never had surgery before the previous night. I was horrified when they explained it is the process of sticking a tube down your throat in order to keep your airway open during surgery. I informed the doctor there was no way I could do that, but I was told, "Patient comfort is not the concern right now, but getting your baby out safely is." He went on to explain that because I'd had surgery the night before, my throat was too swollen and I would need to be awake to help clear my airway should there be complications.

I must say that this is *not* a procedure I would recommend being awake for. It was exceedingly uncomfortable! Both of my arms were stretched out to the side and tied down, while a bite block was placed in my mouth. The intubation tube, although only a half inch in diameter, felt like the size of a fire hose. Every time the tube was inserted into my throat, I would gag, and it felt like my incision from the night before was going to burst. I had very little pain medicine onboard due to my unborn baby. After five tries, they were able to successfully insert the tube, and I was then sedated. Thankfully, we were blessed with a beautiful, healthy baby girl. What an amazing gift from God! I woke up after surgery and saw my husband holding a precious bundle with a little pink cap on. Thank you, God, for her life!

However, my condition after delivery continued to decline, and my platelets continued to drop. The scary thing about HELLP syndrome is there is no guarantee that symptoms will reverse after delivery. The next seventy-two hours were touch and go for me. They drew blood every hour, monitoring my platelets with the hopes that my condition had reversed. My blood levels were becoming dangerously low, and an airlift was ordered to take me to a trauma hospital in Seattle. Thankfully, just before the life flight helicopter landed, my condition reversed. Thank you, God, for sparing my life! We had no idea just how serious this was until it was all over. I have learned since that there have been several women who have died from HELLP syndrome. I felt so blessed to walk away from the ordeal without any long-term organ damage. I have also been so blessed to see my daughter grow into a beautiful woman. What a privilege it has been to be her mother. She and I are best of friends and enjoy so many of the same interests in life.

I believe God allows trials like this to get our attention. When we face our mortality, we are sobered by how fragile life is. It was not long after this my path crossed with my friend Doris. Since those days, God has continued to refine me and has shown me each time that He is in control.

There have been many times in my life when I have questioned God. I have wondered why life can be so hard. I found myself comparing my life to others, wondering why things seem to go so easy for them and so hard for me. I had declared that I wanted Jesus to be the Lord of my life, but so many times during the dark times I questioned what was happening to me. I wanted to take back the control. This letting go and letting God has been a long process for me and still continues. There has been a lot of refining and a lot of sorrowful days. We say we want Him to be Lord, and then when things start to happen that we don't want or like, we start to wonder about the decision to give the reins to God. This is where your will comes up against God's will.

The business paradigm formula I was taught was *knowledge* plus your *paradigm* equals the *results* in life. If we have *superior knowle*dge but are having *inferior results*, then this can cause confusion and frustration. Usually, that is a good sign that there is something wrong with our paradigm. I believe this applies to our spiritual lives as well. We have the Bible, which is the living and holy word of God. It is the best log book ever written. It is the ultimate in *superior knowledge* and is truth. God has given us *everything* we need to know on how to navigate life. If we experience confusion, frustration, and a defeated life when trials come, then there is something wrong with our paradigm regarding who God is and what we believe about Him. A. W. Tozer said, "What I believe about God is the most important thing about me."

Over time, I realized that some of my paradigm was wrong about who God is. I had superior knowledge from the Bible but inferior results. God wanted me to change my paradigm, and He has done it through these trials in my life. He has not done this to hurt me but rather to bless me. I believe that most people who have turned away from God and His plan are the ones who have had a wrong paradigm of Him.

> For this light momentary affliction is preparing for us an eternal weight of glory beyond all comparison. (2 Corinthians 4:17 ESV)

Here are just a few false paradigms that go against what the Bible says, but sadly, many people have these ideas locked in their minds. Then when trials hit, the results can be confusion, anger, and frustration.

False message 1. God is austere and takes us to the woodshed every time we mess up. So often, well-meaning people say, "God is going to get you," or, "God is watching." This message paints God as harsh and austere. With this message lodged in our paradigms, we are fearful of God, and when trials come, we immediately think that He is punishing us or blame Him for all pain and suffering. With this mind-set, it is very easy to get offended at God and turn away from Him. It would be like trying to have a relationship with an abusive parent.

> **Truth.** The Lord does discipline those He loves (Hebrews 12:6), but it is always in love and for our good and blessing. However, not every trial is discipline, but with this false paradigm, we can think it is. Oftentimes, we ask the question, "What did I do wrong?" A better way to express this idea that God is watching us is, "Yes, God is watching me, and He can't get His eyes off of me because He loves me so much." What a paradigm shift.
>
> *Grace* is a foreign way of thinking to a world that operates on laws. The Old Testament in the Bible was based on law, and the punishment for sin was harsh. The New Testament is based on the grace of God because of what Jesus did on the cross in taking on our punishment for sin. We are taught in society that there is punishment for wrong behavior or mistakes. If we mess up in school, we are expelled. If we get bad grades, we fail the class. If we mess up on the job, we are fired. If we break the law, we can go to jail. In God's economy, it's all about grace. If we fail His test, we quite often get to take it over again. He is gracious, loving, and knows our weaknesses and frailty. He is forgiving and full of compassion. He is on our side and wants us to prosper in Him. If we refuse to learn,

then He knows what it will take to turn us around, but it is always done with grace and love.

False message 2. God does not love me and does not care about my needs. He is not interested in each one of us individually. With this mentality, there is no relationship with God but instead a type of religion. When trials come, we often feel alone and unloved by God. This false paradigm creates the question: "How could a loving God allow this?" When something terrible happens, we immediately think God does not love us at all.

> **Truth.** The Lord does love us and desires a personal relationship with each one of us.
>
> God showed how much He loved us by sending His one and only Son into the world so that we might have eternal life through Him. This is real love, not that we loved God, but that He loved us and sent His Son as a sacrifice to take away our sins. (1 John 4:9–10 NLT)
>
> By this we know that we abide in Him, and He in us, because He has given us of His Spirit. (1 John 4:13 NKJV)
>
> The first thing we need to realize is that God has never condoned sin, and sin is the reason for all the evil and horrible things that have happened in this life. Satan is the one who would love for us to put all the blame on God. He is the destroyer of our lives and is raging about seeking whom he may devour. 1 Peter 5:8 (NKJV) says, "Be sober, be vigilant; because your adversary the devil walks about like a roaring lion, seeking whom he may devour." However, Psalm 46:1 (NKJV) says, "God is our refuge and strength, a very present help in trouble." Sin, disease, and death

were conquered by Jesus's death on the cross and His resurrection three days later.

Greater love has no one than this, than to lay down one's life for his friends. (John 15:13 NKJV)

God loves all of us unconditionally, no matter how much we have messed up. He paid an enormous price to buy us back to Himself. He is not harsh and austere, just waiting to bash us down. God wants us to live victoriously above every storm in life, and the only way to do this is by allowing Him to help us.

False message 3. God exists to serve us. We expect Him to drop everything and cater to our every need. Prayer is the vending machine that dispenses whatever we request. Some people think that because their prayers were not answered the way they wanted, God must not exist. We often feel God owes us something.

> **Truth.** We exist to glorify God. We are sinners saved by grace. We belong to Him, and He is almighty, sovereign God.
>
> For you were bought at a price; therefore glorify God in your body and in spirit, which are God's. (1 Corinthians 6:20 NKJV)
>
> Therefore, I urge you, brothers and sisters, in view of God's mercy, to offer your bodies as a living sacrifice, holy and pleasing to God; this is your true and proper worship. (Romans 12:1 NIV)

False message 4. We put limits on what God can do. We put God in our human boxes. We quite often take man's word over God's word. When people say to us there is no hope, we often accept that and then become hopeless.

Truth. With God, there is always hope. He is not bound by human limitations.

The Bible is full of miraculous stories both in the Old and New Testaments. In the New Testament we read of Jesus healing the sick, raising the dead, and casting out demons. One of the greatest miracles is the resurrection of Jesus when He conquered sin, death, and disease.

We may think that He has changed and that His power is no longer available to us anymore. This is simply not true. Miracles still do happen, and nothing is too hard for God.

Ah, Lord God! Behold, You have made the heavens and the earth by Your great power and outstretched arm. There is nothing too hard for You. (Jeremiah 32:17 NKJV)

False message 5. The Bible is no longer valid and is out of date.

Truth. God does not change. "Jesus Christ is the same yesterday, today and forever" (Hebrews 13:8 NKJV). His standards have never changed, and His word is still as current and relevant today as it ever has been. He gives us a standard to live by. He knows what is best for us; after all, He created us.

All scripture is given by inspiration of God, and is profitable for doctrine, for reproof, for correction, for instruction in righteousness. (2 Timothy 3:16 NKJV)

False message 6. Formula Christianity works. This is called performance-based religion and is *works* based. We believe that if we live right, then nothing bad will ever happen to us. If we serve God or give of our time and money, then we think God owes us. With this mentality, we think we can earn our way to heaven. How sad to spend our lives serving with the thought that God will let us into heaven because of what we did here on earth. This performance-based religion goes against everything God says in the Bible.

> **Truth.** Regarding trials in life, we are promised that we will have tribulations. Jesus lived a perfect life and was falsely accused, beaten, spit upon, and then crucified. His life here on earth was full of trials. We as His followers can expect the same.

> "These things I have spoken to you, that in Me you may have peace. In the world you will have tribulation; but be of good cheer, I have overcome the world." (John 16:33 NKJV)

> As far as performance-based living goes, the Bible is very clear that our *good works* are as *filthy rags* and that we are saved by the grace of God not by *works*. We are saved *unto* good works not *by* good works. Ephesians 2:10 (KJV) says, "For we are His workmanship, created in Christ Jesus unto good works, which God hath before ordained that we should walk in them." After we become followers of Jesus, we want to become like Him. Any good works that come out of us happen because He is in us.

> As it is written: "There is none righteous, no, not one. (Romans 3:10 NKJV)

> For all have sinned and fall short of the glory of God, being justified freely by His grace through the redemption that is in Christ Jesus. (Romans 3:23 NKJV)

> But God, who is rich in mercy, because of His great love with which He loved us, even when we were dead in trespasses, made us alive together with Christ … For by grace you have been saved through faith, and that not of yourselves; it is the gift of God, not of works, lest anyone should boast. (Ephesians 2:4–5, 8–9 NKJV)

> But we are all like an unclean thing, and all our righteousness's are like filthy rags. (Isaiah 64:6 NKJV)

There are so many other false paradigms about God that get lodged in our minds and greatly affect how we respond to Him. I have listed some of the most common lies. It is vital to take an inventory of our thoughts and beliefs. If we have a false paradigm about God, it will show up in a trial for sure. It is so important to study the word of God and align our thoughts with His thoughts. This is how we repair our false paradigms about Him. According to John MacArthur, "Being Spirit filled starts with being scripture saturated."

As I got squeezed by the painful events in my life, I realized that my paradigm of God had some inaccuracies. The first thing I thought after finding out that I had a brain tumor was, *What have I done wrong?* I saw God taking me to the woodshed but wasn't sure what I had done to displease Him. I believe it is good to ask God if He is trying to show us something in a trial, but to make the assumption He is beating us is wrong theology.

I also struggled with whether God really loved me. The ordeal I went through in my brain tumor trial clouded my thinking about God's love for me. I had asked Him to change me, not kill me or cripple me. I had invited Him to be Lord of my life, but I did not want to walk through this valley of the shadow of death.

As time went on and I continued to seek God's face, I realized that God was not beating me up but rather taking a crisis that was likely to happen whether I prayed or not and using it to change me and bless me with lessons I would probably never be able to learn any other way. He gently carried me through those dark days and held me close. He spared my life and gave me back the ability to walk and resume a fairly normal lifestyle. He revealed to me through the trial there is so much more to life than what I was focused on. His sheep (His people) were far more important than our cattle.

So often in life, we set goals that are for our advancement, forgetting that God's kingdom is the only one that will last. The Lord reminded me that this life is short and we should not waste it. He also taught me He is in total control of my life and death is not to be feared. It is rather a very huge upgrade for those who know Jesus and follow Him. When our work is done here on earth, we get to graduate to heaven. What a paradigm shift in our view of death.

As the storm clouds persisted and I was faced with breast cancer, God continued to reveal His love for me. I have learned and continue to learn that my feelings are fickle and are not always accurate. I have felt many times in life that God did not love me because of the hard events that He has allowed in my life, but I know from the Bible that He loves me unconditionally. I have experienced His love in so many ways, and I know He cares about me. I have sensed God's presence in my life and seen Him orchestrate events on my behalf. How amazing is that?! The God of this universe cares about everything in my life. God was slowly but surely repairing my paradigm of Himself.

> Casting all your care upon Him for He cares for you.
> (1 Peter 5:7 NKJV)

> For He Himself has said "I will never leave you or forsake you." (Hebrews 13:5 NKJV)

The trials in my life have increased my faith in Him. I once read that the purpose of faith is not always to keep us from trouble but is often to carry us through trouble. If we never experienced trouble, we would not need faith. What we need in the midst of trouble is God's powerful, overcoming grace. He can be trusted with our lives.

Spiritual victory and that abundant life come from abiding in Christ. This is the only way to produce spiritual fruit in our lives that is pleasing to Him. Fruit trees do not stand around trying to grunt out fruit. The branches abide in the tree, and the result is fruit. The same is true for us. We abide in Him, and the result is spiritual fruit. We cannot do life successfully without God's help. We need to allow His lordship and control in our lives to experience the abundant life He died to give us. True victory and the reflection of Himself in our lives comes from stepping out of the way and letting Him flow through us. We let Him pour the water of His word into our earthen vessels, and He turns the water into wine.

> Abide in Me, and I in you. As the branch cannot bear fruit by itself, unless it abides in the vine, neither can you, unless you abide in Me. (John 15:4 ESV)

I believe it is vital to recognize who our enemies are in life. The Bible tells us that we war against the rulers of darkness (Ephesians 6:12). We fight against the world, the flesh, and the devil. John 10:10 says, "Satan comes to steal, kill, and destroy." He is a liar and a deceiver; his goal is to divide and conquer. He would love to take us out and is relentless in his efforts to draw us away from God. He would like to thwart God's purpose for our lives. He wants to get us to doubt scripture. The mind is the first place Satan comes to attack, and he likes to use it as his playground. We need to understand the tactics of the enemy and not give him any access to our lives.

> Satan, who is the god of this world, has blinded the minds of those who don't believe. They are unable to

see the glorious light of the Good News. They don't understand this message about the glory of Christ, who is the exact likeness of God. (2 Corinthians 4:4 NLT)

And do not be conformed to this world, but be transformed by the renewing of your mind, that you may prove what is that good and acceptable and perfect will of God. (Romans 12:2 NKJV)

Once we understand who our enemy is, we need to realize that evil never comes from God. God may allow the problem, but He has the answer to the problem. Trials come to everyone in life. When trials come, we need to realize that God is there to help us, not hurt us. Satan is always our enemy and wants to destroy us. Some of our trials come because we reap what we sow. Others come from the enemy of our souls, and some come because we live in a sin-cursed world where other people's sins can cause us pain. God can use these storms in our lives for blessing if we will let Him. Sometimes He tests us in the storm to refine our character and to strengthen our faith. Other times we are pruned so we will produce more fruit. Like with fruit trees, in order to produce healthy fruit, the *sucker* branches (which are those things that are choking our destinies) have to be pruned. This process is not very pleasant but is necessary. Sometimes these storms are God's way of pruning us.

The last and probably the most important thing that God revealed to me about my damaged paradigm was that He is sovereign. This shift in my paradigm took place during one of the most painful storms of all—the death of my precious sister.

I was raised under the Bible teaching of my dear dad who would often talk about the sovereignty of God. I had this head knowledge, and yet it was greatly tested when my sister passed away. When I was praying for her healing, I had great faith in God's power to heal her. I believed with my whole heart that He was going to answer my prayers. When she died, I was devastated and my faith was shaken.

After a lot of soul searching and quiet time with God, I realized my faith was in what God could do and not in my Savior who knows best. What a revelation for me to discover I was trusting in what God would do for me and not in a sovereign God who does all things right. I am so thankful that God is in complete control. Can you only imagine what a mess we would be in if He was not? He knows everything from the beginning to the end. He knows what is up ahead, and He has a perfect plan. What He wants us to do is trust Him. Trust Him in every decision that He makes on our behalf. He loves us and has good plans for each one of us.

I miss my sister so much, and there are not many days that go by that I don't long to pick up the phone to talk with her or stop in for a cup of coffee. I wish heaven had visiting hours. The pain in my heart is so great, but I know that God's decision to take her to heaven was in His sovereign will and a part of His perfect plan. A very important question we need to ask ourselves is do we worship God for who He is or do we worship God for what we can get?

How can He be Lord of our lives if we don't trust His decisions? Coming to grips with this revelation has greatly changed my view of God and of life. It has given me peace and joy knowing that I am in safe hands. This life here on earth is temporary. James 4:14 (NKJV) says, "For what is your life? It is even a vapor that appears for a little time and then vanishes away." The eternal life to come is where the party begins, and we who have accepted God's plan will all celebrate together with Him.

> Let us rejoice and be glad and give Him glory! For the wedding of the Lamb has come, and His bride has made herself ready. (Revelation 19:7 NIV)

God had a plan for my life, and it did not match the course I was on. It is easy to say we have surrendered, but when we are asked to give up something that is near and dear to our hearts, it is a struggle. I have been tested and tried. I can honestly say that His way is the best way. His pearls are the real deal and last forever. He is worthy of our devotion and praise. He is trustworthy and will never leave us or forsake us. He wants us to simply trust His plan and His heart.

As I was finishing up this book, I took a day off to help with some fencing projects on the ranch. We worked hard all day, and I was tired. We were expecting some pine trees to be delivered, and I thought it would be a good idea to weed whack with the tractor before we planted them. I thought I would do this one last chore before calling it a day. The tractor battery was dead, so I needed to jump-start it. As I climbed up to try and start it for the second time, I lost my footing. It all happened so fast I don't know exactly what I did to cause the accident. The next thing I knew, I was falling fast. I hit the ground hard and broke my left wrist, which required surgery to repair. Here I am sitting in my chair all broken up from my injuries and being tested again.

Twenty-five years ago, my response would have been so much different than it is today. I am very disappointed that I fell and needed surgery, but I am so thankful that I didn't break my neck or get run over by the tractor. I am thankful that I didn't crack my head open or have a brain bleed. I am thankful God is helping me through just like He always has. God reminded me to be thankful *in* the storm, not necessarily *for* the storm. I need to focus on the blessings, not the waves. A thankful heart is a happy heart.

Is there a purpose in the pain? Does God really care for me? Yes, He does! Life is full of storms and black clouds. He wants me to trust Him and believe in His goodness. I'm not going to get all the answers, and there are a million things we will never understand. We have to give up the right to know. He wants me to trust Him. He is not hurting me but rather helping me. He is preparing me for a fabulous new life to come. He wants me to abide in Him and let Him handle all the stress of life.

> I can do all things through Christ who strengthens me. (Philippians 4:13 NKJV)

I either believe the Bible, or I don't. If I believe it, then I need to believe all of it and not just take the parts I want or need. God's word, the Bible, is the only true instruction manual for life. It is His love letter to us. Do you believe the word of God enough to live by it? I do!

> "For whoever desires to save his life will lose it, but whoever loses his life for My sake will find it. For what profit is it to a man if he gains the whole world, and loses his own soul? Or what will a man give in exchange for his soul?"
> —Matthew 16:25-26 (NKJV)

I Have Been Through the Valley of Weeping

By L. B. Cowan

> When He leads through some valley of trouble,
> His omnipotent hand we trace;
> For the trials and sorrows He sends us,
> Are part of His lessons in grace.

SECTION 4
ANCHOR OF HOPE

This hope we have as an anchor of the soul, both sure and steadfast, and which enters the Presence behind the veil.

—Hebrews 6:19 (NKJV)

THE SIPHON

For the wages of sin is death, but the gift of God is
eternal life in Christ Jesus our Lord.

—Romans 6:23 (NKJV)

While we lived in Central Washington, we ran our cattle on a beautiful
ranch that was bordered by a very large irrigation canal, often referred
to as the siphon. It was a cement channel that ran for several miles and
then fed into a giant culvert that was probably fifty feet in diameter. It
was called the *sheep dip*, and it was where all that water from the canal
flowed down the hill and under the road. There was quite a drop in
elevation, so the pressure and the volume of water passing through the
pipe were tremendous.

One day while out checking the cattle, I had crossed this canal and
was heading back home. A young woman in a pickup truck stopped
me and asked if I had seen her dogs. She had lost track of them and
was unfamiliar with the area. She had turned her dogs loose to let them
run. I had not seen them but told her I would keep my eyes open for
them. I also warned her of the canal and its danger.

I drove away and climbed the hill with a bird's-eye view of the canal
below. As I was surveying the landscape, my eyes caught sight of two
black dots in the water, and my heart sank. Her dogs were Labrador
retrievers and were naturally drawn to the water. I flagged her down
and told her we had only about a mile to save them because if they
reached the sheep dip, it would be too late. We parked our trucks and

began to run alongside the canal, calling out to the dogs with the hope they would come close to the pull-out areas on either side. At each pull-out they would be on the opposite side of the canal, and we could not get our hands on them. The water running through the canal was flowing so fast I didn't dare get in and try to save them. I ran the full mile alongside the dogs but was unable to make contact.

I will never forget watching those two magnificent black labs enter that huge cement culvert. They were swimming along so oblivious to the danger, doing what they loved best. Inside the siphon it was dark, and the waters churned violently. It was incredibly sad to watch the beautiful heads of those two gorgeous dogs being sucked down into the violent waters of that siphon. I knew they would never survive the fall. Even if they could have held their breath, the pressure of the water would crush them. It was a sight that is hard to forget, and it made me sick to my stomach.

I had outrun the owner of these dogs, and as I walked back to tell her the horrible news, I was gripped by the thought of what it would be like to be oblivious to the eternal damnation for those that reject God's plan of salvation. Just like these dogs, there are so many people floating through life ignoring all the warning signs of what's ahead for them if they reject Christ. The Bible clearly states there is judgment coming, and the way to avoid eternal destruction is through the cross of Christ.

I once had a guy tell me that he was going to live like crazy and then accept Christ just before he died. I responded, "I hope you have time." So many times people's lives end without warning. Look at how quickly life changed for those people who were killed in the twin trade towers on 9/11. Life that morning was fairly normal for most of them as they went off to work. Who of us would have ever imagined those towers were going to go down that day! Similarly, mass shootings happen without warning, or people have accidents or medical emergencies. None of us are guaranteed we will have time to process or think before we die. Now is the time to think about it and be prepared.

It reminds me of a story I heard about an eagle floating on a big block of ice in the river. He floated right up to the falls, thinking he would fly away as the block went over the edge only to find out that his feet were frozen to the ice and he was unable to free himself as he plummeted to his death.

> Behold, now is the accepted time; behold, now is the day of salvation. (2 Corinthians 6:2 NKJV)

There are so many people floating through life who do not believe in God at all. Some choose to believe in evolution, thinking we just die like animals. What a rude awakening lies ahead for these poor souls. How terrifying to be sucked down the siphon and go into a lost eternity apart from God. The harsh reality for them is that their belief does not change what God's word says is going to happen.

There are other people in the canal of life who believe in God but have never accepted Him as Savior. They are offended at Him because something terrible has happened to them and they blame Him for it. They would rather hold onto bitterness than receive forgiveness. Sometimes these people might even say there is no God, but in reality, they know He exists and are just angry at Him. Perhaps it is because they are living a lifestyle they know God says is wrong. The Bible is full of guidelines on how to live. God created us and has given us His instruction manual to live by. There are others who say the Bible is so out of date and God's ways are old-fashioned and ridiculous. The Bible is still true and very relevant for us today. God has never changed. The problems come when people think they know better than God and re-create their own rules and regulations.

Another category of people in the canal of life are those who think because they go to church or because they live in a Christian country or were raised in a Christian home that they are Christians and will go to heaven. That is kind of like saying, "If I go out and sit in the barn, I will become a horse." That is not how becoming a follower of Christ works. We have to make it personal by confessing with our mouths and believing in our hearts. These people acknowledge that God exists and it all sounds good, but they have never made it personal. This would be like floating by the sign along the canal that reads, "Danger Ahead—GET OUT!" and saying, "That is a good sign, and I'm sure it is true," but then not paying attention to the warning.

> If you confess with your mouth that Jesus is Lord and believe in your heart that Jesus is Lord and believe in your heart that God raised Him from the dead, you will be saved. For it is by believing in your heart that you are made right with God, and it is by confessing with your mouth that you are saved. (Romans 10:9–10 NLT)

Another group of people floating in the canal are those who care more about what others think than what God thinks. They do not want others to see them as weak or weird. Sadly, they would rather have the approval of man than please God. They hope there is going to be a party in hell. I had a guy tell me once that he didn't want to go to heaven because his dad wasn't going to be there. There will be no reconnecting in hell. It is eternal separation from God and is referred to as the furnace of fire where there will be wailing and gnashing of teeth (Matthew 13:50).

> And do not fear those who kill the body but cannot kill the soul. But rather fear Him who is able to destroy both soul and body in hell. (Matthew 10:28 NKJV)

What a sad thing to be heading for the siphon and not know it. This brings me to the last group in the dangerous canal—those who follow a false religion. How incredibly sad to die after a life of service to their religion and find out they were following the wrong way. There is only one way that we come to God, and it is through Jesus, who said, "I am the way, the truth, and the life. No one comes to the Father except through Me" (John 14:6 NKJV). What a bummer to find out this life was the only heaven they will experience. This life on earth with all its sin, destruction, disease, and death is a far cry from the beauty and perfection of heaven.

Matthew 7:21–23 (NKJV) says, "Not everyone who says to Me, 'Lord, Lord,' shall enter the kingdom of heaven, but he who does the will of My Father in heaven. Many will say to Me in that day, 'Lord, Lord, have we not prophesied in Your name, cast out demons in Your name, and done many wonders in Your name?' And then I will declare to them, 'I never knew you; depart from Me, you who practice lawlessness!'"

These verses apply to the religions out there that do not follow God's word and have followed man's way instead. They have either abandoned the Bible completely or added or subtracted to God's plan with their own rules and regulations.

> All roads lead to God but only one road leads to heaven, and that's the road through Jesus Christ!
> (Greg Laurie)

These false religions are just another one of Satan's schemes to kill, steal, and destroy. They use the same words but a different dictionary. My dad use to say, "When God is doing something good, Satan loves to set up housekeeping right next door." Satan loves to imitate what God is doing, and he makes it look like the real thing when it is counterfeit. Some people have been deceived into believing that God's free gift of salvation is not enough and our good works will make up the difference. They acknowledge that Jesus died on the cross but add the part that feeds the pride of man and teach that we can earn our way by doing all the good we can. This supposes what Jesus did on the cross for us was not enough and we will be acceptable to God by our own righteousness.

Now this may sound harsh and be very offensive to some if this is how they have been taught to believe. Yet God's word is very clear on the fact that there is only one way to heaven. If someone I loved or cared about was floating in this canal headed toward the siphon, I would hopefully be pleading with him or her to get out before the upcoming danger. I was panicked to try and help those two dogs get out. How much more important it is to help those who have souls that will live after death.

Jesus spoke a parable about this in Matthew 13:24–30 (NKJV):

> Another parable He put forth to them saying: "The kingdom of heaven is like a man who sowed good seed in his field; but while men slept, his enemy came and sowed tares among the wheat and went his way. But when the grain had sprouted and produced a crop, then the tares also appeared. So the servants of the owner came and said to him, 'Sir, did you not sow good seed in your field? How then does it have tares?' He said to them, 'An enemy has done this.' The servants said to him, 'Do you want us then to go and gather them up?' But he said 'No, lest while you gather up the tares you also uproot the wheat with them. Let both grow together until the harvest, and at the time of harvest I will say to the reapers, First gather together the tares and bind them in bundles to burn them, but gather the wheat into my barn.'"

Some translations refer to the tares as darnel seeds, a weed that resembles wheat. Satan is subtle and loves to deceive. He desires to drive people away from God, and he sows darnel seeds that look like the truth but are really false. All through scripture it is very clear that there is only one way to heaven, and that is through Jesus Christ. This is God's way—not man's.

> Jesus said to him, "I am the way, the truth, and the life. No one comes to the Father except through Me." (John 14:6 NKJV)

> For by grace you have been saved through faith, and
> that not of yourselves; it is the gift of God, not of
> works, lest anyone should boast. (Ephesians 2:8–9
> NKJV)

Jesus desires to have a personal relationship with each one of us. He desires to be our Guide, our Counselor, our Savior, and our Friend. God's plan of salvation is simple. It is a free gift to us, and all that is required is that we turn toward Him and receive His forgiveness by confessing our sins and our need of Him.

The Bible is the inspired word of God, and it is the only book that tells us of God's plan to rescue fallen sinful human beings from sin and hopelessness. There are endless proofs that God's word is true and infallible. Why would anyone think they could add to or subtract from what God says? He is God! He is all-knowing and perfect in every way. Why would we even dare to think we could improve or change what He says to be true? Only in our pride and arrogance do we resist the love and mercy of God so beautifully expressed to us in the Bible.

The Bible is also a book where the many prophecies given have come to pass. We will find a prophesy as to where Jesus would be born and the kind of death He would die, along with so many others that can be studied by those who want to know the validity of God's holy word. There are still some prophecies to be fulfilled, and one of those is what Bible scholars call the rapture. It is the promise of Jesus coming again to rapture out of this world His true followers. No one knows when the rapture will take place, but it is something that is imminent and definite. 2 Timothy 3:1–5 talks about what it will be like in the last days, and by all indications, we are experiencing them even now. As believers in Jesus Christ, we look forward to the rapture.

> For the Lord Himself will descend from heaven with
> a shout, with the voice of an archangel, and with the
> trumpet of God. And the dead in Christ will rise first.

> Then we who are alive and remain shall be caught up together with them in the clouds to meet the Lord in the air. And thus we shall always be with the Lord. Therefore comfort one another with these words. (1 Thessalonians 4:16–18 NKJV)

After the rapture takes place, then comes the great tribulation, which is spoken of in the books of Daniel and Revelation and lasts for seven years. Next on God's timetable is the second coming of Christ when He comes back to judge the earth, and His followers will come back with Him. What an amazing thought and comfort it is to know that we who know Him are on the winning side.

If you are reading this book and you are not sure what you believe, it is my prayer that you will consider the truth about God and His salvation. Are you floating in the canal of life headed for destruction? We all need to ask, "Does what I believe line up with what God says in His word, the Bible?" Are you willing to gamble on where you are going to spend eternity? If what you are being taught or what you believe goes against what the Bible teaches, then please pay close attention. This is not something anyone of us should be careless with.

Life can end so quickly, and then it is too late to correct your belief system. Once you die, the Bible says your destiny is fixed. Someday each one of us will stand before God, and we will either present Christ's righteousness or our own.

> There is a way that seems right to a man, but its end is the way of death. (Proverbs 14:12 NKJV)

I am so thankful that when we accept God's plan of salvation that our sins are permanently forgiven and removed as far as the east is from the west (Psalm 103:12). When Jesus took our punishment on the cross, He wiped out our past, present, and future sins. We are forgiven completely and have an eternal home in heaven waiting for us. When we accept

His plan of salvation, it is like being lifted out of the siphon. We are no longer headed for eternal separation from God. If you do not know this Jesus of mine, I beg you to invite Him into your life today. Grab hold of the lifeline He is throwing you, and get out of the dangerous canal that flows straight into hell.

The most serious sin is to reject God's plan of salvation. This is the sin of unbelief, and it is the only sin that cannot be forgiven. There is no sin that God will not forgive except the sin of rejecting His Son. If we refuse to accept His plan of salvation, we will be faced with the punishment of our sins. A loving God is not willing that any should perish (2 Peter 3:9). If we choose to ignore His offer, we will be trampling over His blood on the way to a lost eternity. The choice is ours, and it is the most important decision we will ever make. It is truly a matter of life or death.

> For the wages of sin is death, but the free gift of God is eternal life through Christ Jesus our Lord. (Romans 6:23 NLT)

A Voice from Hell

by Oscar C. Eliason

"Oh, why am I here in this place of unrest
When others have entered the land of the blest?
God's way of salvation was preached unto men;
I heard it and heard it, again and again.

Why did I not listen and turn from my sin
And open my heart and let Jesus come in?
For vain earthly pleasures my soul did I sell—
The way I had chosen has brought me to hell.

I wish I were dreaming, but ah, it is true.
The way to be saved I had heard and I knew;

My time on the earth, oh, so quickly fled by,
How little I thought of the day I would die.

When God's Holy Spirit was pleading with me,
I hardened my heart and I turned from His plea.
The way that was sinful, the path that was wide,
I chose and I walked till the time that I died.

Eternally now, I must dwell in this place.
If I from my memory could but erase
The thoughts of my past which are haunting me so.
Oh, where is a refuge to which I can go?

This torture and suff'ring, how long can I stand?
For Satan and devils this only was planned.
God's refuge is Jesus, the One that I spurned;
He offered salvation, but from Him I turned.

My brothers and sisters I wish I could warn.
Far better 'twould be if I had not been born.
The price I must pay is too horrid to tell—
My life without God led directly to Hell."

Oh, soul without Christ, will these words be your cry?
God's Word so declares it that all men must die.
From hell and its terrors, Oh, flee while you may!
So come to the Saviour; He'll save you today!

WHAT IS YOUR EXIT STRATEGY?

He who has the Son has life; he who does not have the
Son of God does not have life.

—1 John 5:12 (NKJV)

Carl McCunn was a photographer who in the spring of 1981 paid
a bush pilot to take him to a remote lake approximately 225 miles
northeast of Fairbanks, Alaska, near the Coleen River in the Alaskan
wilderness. Carl was an experienced outdoorsman and had taken
this trip several times before. On this particular trip, he intended to
photograph wildlife for about five months, so, as in times past, he hired
a bush pilot to fly him in and drop him off. He had calculated all his
needs and knew how many rolls of film, matches, food, ammunition,
journals, and other supplies that he needed for the five months he
would spend alone. However, he somehow failed to confirm with the
pilot where he was to be picked up. After the five months were past,
when the expected plane had not arrived, he wrote in his diary, "I think
I should have used more foresight about arranging my departure."

As the days continued and the weather started to turn cold, Carl feared
that he would not be found, so he began rationing his remaining
supplies. By November, he was suffering from frostbite and starvation.
Sometime between late November and early December, Carl wrote a
letter to his father, pinned his Alaska driver's license to the note, and
shot himself. Just before his suicide, he wrote in his diary, "They say
it doesn't hurt." The following spring Carl was found in his tent along

with all of his film and his hundred-page diary. Carl was only thirty-five years old at the time of his death.

Somehow in all the planning of this adventure, Carl had overlooked the most important part of his plan. We think, *How in the world could this even happen?* And yet, isn't that like most of us? We have our lives all calculated out with short term and long term goals. We might have the college funds figured out for our children, a nice padded savings account, and a retirement plan in place along with a will but so often we don't take time to think out the exit strategy!

A very sobering statistic for each person alive is this: one out of one is going to die. Life as we know it will end for every single one of us. Nobody ever wants to talk about his or her death or even think about it because it seems so morbid. The inevitable will happen someday, but we say, "I will think about that some other day," and we keep putting it off. How horrible to end up like Carl did with the agonizing fact that with some foresight and planning, he could have been picked up and flown out to safety.

Sickness and tragedy have a way of making us stop to analyze our lives. An accident, a heart attack, or a stroke can take away your ability to function normally or can end your life. We do not all die of old age. We do not all get to say our goodbyes and prepare. Sometimes it is without warning like it was for those who went to work in the Trade Center towers that tragic September 11. Corrie Ten Boom put it well when she said, "Standing in front of a crematorium, knowing that any day could be your last day, gives one a different perspective on life."

I once had a neighbor who told me he feels we just cease to be, and our souls die when our hearts stop beating. The Bible tells us differently and says our souls will live for all eternity. What a horrible thing to die without Christ and wake up in hell knowing we could have chosen heaven.

Jesus said, "I am the resurrection and the life. He who believes in Me, though he may die, he shall live. And whoever lives and believes in Me shall never die" (John 11:25–26 NKJV).

The Bible also states that everyone will stand before God someday and give an account for his or her life. Hebrews 9:27 (NKJV) says, "It is appointed unto men once to die, but after this the judgment." That judgment will be terrifying for those who have not accepted God's plan of salvation.

John 3:15—18 (NLT) says, "That everyone who believes in Him (Jesus) will have eternal life. For God loved the world so much, that He gave His one and only Son, that everyone who believes in Him will not perish, but have eternal life. God sent his Son into the world not to judge the world, but to save the world through Him. There is no judgment against anyone who believes in Him. But anyone who does not believe in Him has already been judged for not believing in God's one and only Son."

John 5:24 (ESV) says, "Truly, truly I say to you, whoever hears My word and believes Him who sent me has eternal life. He does not come into judgment, but has passed from death to life." This is awesome news! Why would anyone not want this? Why would anyone gamble on where he or she is going to spend eternity? Why not map out our exit strategy and choose God's way instead of Satan's lie?

There was an epitaph on a one-hundred-year-old grave that read:

> Pause stranger when you pass me by,
> As you are now so once was I
> As I am now so you will be
> Prepare for death and follow me.

An unknown passerby read those words and scratched this reply:

> To follow you I'm not content,

Until I know which way you went.

Accepting God's free gift of salvation is very simple and does not require good works, church attendance, or any of the other man-made ideas. One of the thieves who was crucified next to Jesus, after confessing that he was a sinner, simply said to Jesus, "Lord, remember me when You come into Your kingdom." Jesus's response to him was, "Assuredly, I say to you, today you will be with Me in Paradise" (Luke 23:42–43 NKJV). All this thief had to do was confess that he was a sinner and repent. He recognized that Jesus was his Savior and cried out for mercy, and he was saved.

If we have accepted Jesus as our Savior, then heaven awaits us after this life, and that is when the party begins. Heaven is going to be amazing. The Bible says, "No eye has seen, no ear has heard, and no mind has imagined what God has prepared for those who love Him" (1 Corinthians 2:9 NLT). What an amazing thing it will be to enter heaven and see Jesus face-to-face—to feel His embrace and hear His voice. To know that we will live forever with Him in a sinless environment—in perfect bodies free of pain, disease, and sorrow. There will be no more disappointments, no more heartaches, and no more goodbyes. It will be a place of perfect peace and contentment. It will be paradise!

For those who have been trapped in bodies that are deformed or permanently damaged, they will be made new, and some will walk or see for the first time. We will all have our new resurrected bodies with perfected minds, and we will be free of our sinful nature. Heaven, unlike hell, is a place to reconnect with loved ones who have gone on before. Can you even imagine the reunions that await us? I am looking forward to seeing my two children, my sister, and my parents, along with many other loved ones who have gone before me.

God created this world and the wonders of the universe—the stars and all the galaxies. Creation is so beautiful, and He has said we haven't seen anything yet. I believe that the music and the sounds of heaven are going to be incredible. I do not for a minute think that heaven will be boring. I believe it will be an amazingly beautiful and exciting place, and we will be full of praise and worship to our resurrected Savior who died to deliver us. He is our light, and there will be no shadows in heaven. It is going to be amazing, and I hope I see you there!

And there shall be no more curse, but the throne of God and of the Lamb shall be in it, and His servants shall serve Him. They shall see His face, and His name shall be on their foreheads. There shall be no night there: They need no lamp nor light of the sun, for the Lord God gives them light. And they shall reign forever and ever.

—Revelation 22:3–5 (NKJV)

It Will Be Worth it All

by Esther K. Rusthoi

It will be worth it all
when we see Jesus!
Life's trials will seem so small
when we see Christ.
One glimpse of his dear face,
all sorrow will erase.
So, bravely run the race
till we see Christ.

Printed in the United States
By Bookmasters